ESSENTIAL
SOCCER
SKILLS

ESSENTIAL SOCCER SKILLS

KEY TIPS AND TECHNIQUES TO IMPROVE YOUR GAME

Includes content previously published in *The Soccer Book*

LONDON, NEW YORK, MUNICH,
MELBOURNE, and DELHI

Senior Editor Bob Bridle
Senior Art Editor Sharon Spencer

Production Editor Tony Phipps
Production Controller Louise Minihane
Jacket Designer Mark Cavanagh

Managing Editor Stephanie Farrow
Managing Art Editor Lee Griffiths

US Editor Margaret Parrish

DK INDIA

Managing Art Editor Ashita Murgai
Editorial Lead Saloni Talwar
Senior Art Editor Rajnish Kashyap
Project Designer Anchal Kaushal
Project Editor Garima Sharma
Designers Amit Malhotra, Diya Kapur
Editors Shatarupa Chaudhari, Karisma Walia
Production Manager Pankaj Sharma
DTP Manager Balwant Singh
Senior DTP Designer Harish Aggarwal
DTP Designers Shanker Prasad, Bimlesh Tiwari, Vishal Bhatia, Jaypal Singh Chauhan
Managing Director Aparna Sharma

First American Edition, 2011

Published in the United States by
DK Publishing
375 Hudson Street
New York, New York 10014
11 12 13 14 15 10 9 8 7 6 5 4 3 2 1

001—176109—Mar/2011

Includes content previously published in
The Soccer Book

Copyright © 2011 Dorling Kindersley Limited
All rights reserved.
No part of this publication may be reproduced, stored in a retrieval system, or transmitted in any form or by any means, electronic, mechanical, photocopying, recording, or otherwise without the prior written permission of the copyright owners.

Published in Great Britain by
Dorling Kindersley Limited.
A catalog record for this book
is available from the Library of Congress.

ISBN 978-0-7566-5902-8

DK books are available at special discounts when urchased in bulk for sales promotions, premiums, -raising, or educational use. For details, contact: ublishing Special Markets, 375 Hudson Street, rk, New York 10014 or SpecialSales@dk.com.

Printed and bound by
Printing Company Limited, China

over more at www.dk.com

Contents

Introduction

Soccer is the most popular sport in the world. From the Andes to Greenland, people just can't seem to resist kicking a leather ball around or watching others doing the same. The figures are staggering—approximately 250 million people play the game regularly. In fact, if soccer players made up a nation, it would be the fourth most populous on the planet.

❝ IF ALL THE SOCCER PLAYERS IN THE WORLD WERE TO FORM A NATION, IT WOULD BE THE FOURTH MOST POPULOUS ON THE PLANET. ❞

You could almost say that soccer is a universal language. If you found yourself in a strange country with no knowledge of the local tongue, you would still be able to strike up a conversation by using a few hand gestures accompanied by the names of some prominent players. Place one hand at chest level while saying "Pelé," then raise it with the word "Maradona" and you'll quickly start making friends.

An interesting observation often made about soccer is that its language is couched in military terms (such as campaigns, tactics, and captains). Some theories claim that soccer is a surrogate for hunting—on which, of course, our ancestors depended for their survival. According to this view, a goal scored is equivalent to a kill, which would certainly explain the sense of importance surrounding the game. Another possibility is that soccer is a kind of ritualized warfare. It may be no accident that its popularity has coincided with an era in which young men have been less regularly engaged in war than in the past. Both these theories have their merits but perhaps another, simpler explanation needs to be added.

Our history can be seen as the story of an ever-increasing split between our physical selves and our minds. Soccer, however, works the other way around. By uniting the brain with the parts of the body at the opposite extremity (the feet), it temporarily heals the split. When we play the game or identify with others who are doing so, we become whole again. And, of course, it is not just men who feel this way. The women's game is extremely popular as well—for every reference to a "he" in this book, a "she" can and should just as easily be substituted.

Essential Soccer Skills celebrates the sport by presenting its varied and complex skills in a clear and simple way. It describes the relative merits of zonal and man-to-man marking, for example, and explains how to perform the perfect header. The book goes on to unravel the complexities of the offside rule and even shows you how to spin and turn like Zinédine Zidane or "bend" the ball like David Beckham. *Essential Soccer Skills* will help you appreciate what makes soccer such a great game to watch—and play.

❝ BY UNITING THE BRAIN AND THE FEET, SOCCER TEMPORARILY HEALS THE SPLIT BETWEEN OUR PHYSICAL AND MENTAL SELVES. ❞

"Some people believe football (soccer) is a matter of life and death," the great Liverpool manager Bill Shankly once said. "I am very disappointed with that attitude. I can assure you it is much, much more important than that." No one has better captured the irrational depth of passion aroused by twenty-two men chasing a ball.

The Basics

The rules

The Laws of the Game were devised by the FA in 1863. As a testament to the game's simplicity, there are only 17 laws in place today. The offside rules (see pp.18–19) have proved to be the most complex to create and administer, having been overhauled three times in the rulebook's history.

Enforcing the rules

The Laws of the Game are enforced by the referee (see pp.22–23), who has the final say in any match disputes. Since 1992, FIFA has stipulated that all referees in international matches must speak English. The referee may be helped by two assistant referees and a fourth official (see pp.24–27). The fourth official is increasingly used in international matches and the leading leagues, primarily to assist the referee in administrative duties.

> **❝ THE OFFSIDE RULE** HAS BEEN OVERHAULED **THREE TIMES** IN THE **RULEBOOK'S HISTORY**. ❞

ROBERTO TROTTA

Former Argentinian defender Roberto Trotta holds the dubious honor of receiving the most red cards. He was sent off a record-breaking 17 times during his career.

Laws of the Game

 11

THE BASICS | THE RULES

1. FIELD OF PLAY

The field (see pp.38–39) must be a rectangle, marked with touchlines, goal lines and areas, a halfway line, a center circle, penalty areas, spots, and arcs, corner arcs, and flag posts. It must be between 100–131yd (90–120m) long and between 49–98yd (45–90m) wide. For international soccer, the limits are 109–120yd (100–110m) and 70–82yd (64–75m), respectively.

2. THE BALL

The ball (see pp.34–35) must be made of approved materials. At the start of the game, it must have a diameter of 27–28in (68.5–71cm), weigh between $14^{1}/_{2}$–16oz (410–450g), and have an internal pressure of between 0.6 and 1.1 atmospheres at sea level. It can only be changed by the referee. If it bursts during a game, play is stopped and restarted with a new drop ball.

3. NUMBER OF PLAYERS

A match consists of two teams of not more than 11 players, each including a goalkeeper. An outfield player may swap with the goalkeeper during a stoppage of play. Teams must have at least seven players to begin or continue a match. In official competitions, a maximum of three player substitutions may be made by each team.

4. PLAYERS' EQUIPMENT

Compulsory equipment for players are a shirt, shorts, socks, shin pads, and soccer shoes or cleats (see pp.28–31). Goalkeepers must wear a uniform that distinguishes them from their own team, their opponents, and the officials. Headgear is allowed if it does not present a threat to other players. Most forms of jewelry are not permitted.

5. THE REFEREE

The referee (see pp.22–23) is the final arbiter and interpreter of the rules. He decides whether a game can go ahead or not, and may stop play if a player requires medical treatment. He cautions players (yellow card), sends them off (red card), and is responsible for timekeeping, record-keeping, and ensuring that all match equipment and uniforms are correct.

6. ASSISTANT REFEREES

The assistant referees (see p.24–25), formerly called linesmen, support the referee, primarily by signaling for corner kicks, throw-ins, and offside infringements. They must also bring the referee's attention to any other fouls or infringements that the referee may not have seen. However, the referee's word is always final.

Laws of the Game (continued)

7. DURATION OF MATCH

There are two equal halves of 45 minutes of play. Additional time may also be added—at the discretion of the referee—in case of injuries, substitutions, and time-wasting. Time can also be added to allow a penalty to be taken at the end of normal time. Rules covering extra time are made by the national soccer associations and confederations.

8. START/RESTART OF PLAY

A coin is tossed at the start of play; the winners choose ends for the first half and the losers kick off. The other team kicks off in the second half. The kick-off is taken from the center spot and the ball must move into the oppositions' half. All players must be in their own half, and the opposition must be at least 10yd (9.15m) away from the ball. The ball must be touched by a second player before the first player can touch it again.

9. BALL IN AND OUT OF PLAY

The ball is in play when it is inside the field of play and the referee has still not stopped play. The ball is out of play when it has completely crossed the sidelines or the goal lines, whether in the air or on the ground. If the ball rebounds off a goalpost, crossbar, corner flagpost, or the referee or one of the assistant referees, and remains in the field of play, it is still in play.

10. METHOD OF SCORING

A goal is scored when the ball has completely crossed the goal line between the goalposts and under the crossbar, provided that no other infringements have taken place. The team with the most goals wins. If both teams score the same number of goals, or if no goals are scored at all, the match is declared as a draw.

11. OFFSIDE

A player is offside (see pp.18–19), at the moment a ball is passed forward, when he is: in the opponents' half of the field; is closer to the opponents' goal line than the ball; and there are fewer than two defenders (including the goalkeeper) closer to the goal line than the attacking player. When a player is called offside, the opposition is awarded a free-kick.

12. FOULS AND MISCONDUCT

A foul (see pp.20–21) has been committed if a player: trips, kicks, pushes, or charges another player recklessly; strikes, attempts to strike, or spits at an opponent; makes a tackle but connects with the player before the ball; deliberately handles the ball (goalkeepers in their area excepted); or obstructs an opponent or prevents them from releasing the ball.

13. FREE-KICKS

Free-kicks (see pp.14–17, 110–13) restart play after a foul or infringement and are usually taken from the place from which the offense was committed. Free-kicks can be "direct," in which the taker may score directly, or "indirect," in which the taker and a second player from the same team must touch the ball before a goal can be scored.

14. PENALTY-KICK

A penalty-kick (see pp.15, 114–17) is awarded for a foul committed by a defending player in his or her own penalty area. The kick is taken from the penalty spot and all other players—except for the goalkeeper and taker—must be at least 10yd (9.15m) from the spot. The taker may touch the ball if it rebounds from the goalkeeper, but not if it rebounds from the post or crossbar.

15. THE THROW-IN

A throw-in (see pp.15, 106–09) is awarded when the ball has crossed the sideline and an opposition player was the last to touch it. The throw is taken from the point from which the ball crossed the line. The taker must have both his feet on the ground, use two hands, throw the ball from behind and over his head, and be facing the field of play.

16. GOAL-KICK

A goal-kick (see pp.118–25) is awarded to the defending team when the ball crosses its goal line, a goal has not been scored, and the last player to touch it was from the opposition. Any player may take the goal-kick, placing the ball anywhere in the goal area. The kick must send the ball out of the penalty area or be retaken. The taker may not touch the ball again until it has been touched by a second player.

17. CORNER-KICK

A corner (see pp.15, 106–09) is awarded to the attacking team when the opposition is last to touch the ball and the ball crosses the goal line without a goal being scored. A corner is also awarded if the ball enters the goal from a throw-in or indirect free-kick. The attacking team restarts play by placing the ball in the corner arc nearest to where it crossed the goal line.

SEEING RED
Law 5 says that the referee's decision is always final.

Using set pieces

A **set piece is a predetermined**, fixed move to restart play when the referee is forced to halt the game temporarily. There are three occasions when a game of soccer is stopped: following an infringement, such as a foul or an offside; when the ball goes out of play; and following a player injury or other interruption, such as a burst ball.

Types of set piece

There are six different types of set piece: goal-kicks, free-kicks, throw-ins, penalty-kicks, corner-kicks, and drop-balls. Free-kicks can be either "direct" or "indirect" (see p.110). In either situation, every member of the opposing team must be at least 10yd (9.15m) from the ball at the moment the kick is taken.

A goal-kick is taken from inside the goal area

GOAL-KICK
A goal-kick is awarded to a defending team when the ball completely crosses the goal line—either on the ground or in the air—having been kicked by an opposing player without a goal being scored.

The goalkeeper organizes the defenders into a wall

FOR FREE-KICKS, EVERY MEMBER OF THE OPPOSING TEAM MUST BE **AT LEAST 10YD (9.15M) FROM THE BALL** WHEN THE **KICK IS TAKEN**.

FREE-KICK
Direct free-kicks are awarded for serious offenses, such as kicking, tripping, or pushing, while indirect free-kicks are awarded for less serious offenses, such as obstruction or offside (see p.16).

The taker kicks the ball from where the infringement took place

THROW-IN

A throw-in is awarded against the team that last touches the ball before it crosses the sideline. It is made with both feet on or behind the sideline, and both hands moving from behind the taker's head.

The thrower must face the field of play and have both feet on the ground

PENALTY-KICK

A penalty is awarded for any offense committed inside the penalty area that would otherwise be punished by a direct free-kick if it had taken place outside the penalty area.

There can be huge pressure on the taker of a penalty-kick, especially during a penalty shootout (see p.114)

Many goals are scored from corners, often as a result of headers

CORNER-KICK

A corner-kick is awarded when the whole ball crosses the goal line (either on ground or in air) having last been touched by a member of the defending team, including the goalkeeper.

The keeper must decide whether to defend from the goal line or advance to try and clear the ball

Set-piece etiquette

If a player is injured, the team in possession is expected to kick the ball into touch. The other side should then return it from the resulting set piece. During an English FA Cup tie in 1999, Sheffield United's goalkeeper kicked the ball out of play so that an injured teammate could receive treatment. But instead of returning the ball, Arsenal midfielder Ray Parlour initiated a move that led to the winning goal. The match was eventually replayed.

DROP-BALL

A drop-ball is played when a game needs to be started again following an incident that is not covered in the rules, such as a serious player injury. When such a case occurs, the ball is not awarded to either team. Instead, a player from one team stands opposite a player from the other team and the referee drops the ball between them.

> **❝ A DROP-BALL IS PLAYED WHEN THE GAME NEEDS TO BE RESTARTED AND THE BALL IS NOT AWARDED TO EITHER TEAM. ❞**

OFFENSES: DIRECT FREE-KICKS

Direct free-kicks are usually awarded for relatively serious offenses (see pp.20–21). The most common are:

KICKING AND TRIPPING
It is an offense for a player to kick or trip—or attempt to kick or trip— an opponent.

JUMPING OR CHARGING
It is an offense for a player to jump or charge at an opponent.

STRIKING AND PUSHING
It is an offense for a player to strike, push, hold, or spit at an opponent.

MAKING CONTACT
It is an offense for a player to touch an opponent before touching the ball when making a tackle.

HANDLING THE BALL
It is an offense for a player to deliberately handle the ball (except for the goalkeeper in his area).

OFFENSES: INDIRECT FREE-KICKS

Indirect free-kicks are usually awarded for less serious offenses than direct free-kicks. The most common are:

OBSTRUCTION
It is an offense for a player to deliberately impede the progress of an opponent.

DANGEROUS PLAY
It is an offense to make an attempt to kick the ball when an opponent is attempting to head it, for example.

IMPEDING THE GOALKEEPER
It is an offense to prevent the goalkeeper from releasing the ball.

TOUCHING THE BALL TWICE
It is an offense to touch the ball twice at a set piece without an intervening touch from another player.

OFFSIDE
If a player is offside (see pp.18–19), an indirect free-kick is given to the opposition.

High stakes

Since many goals are scored from set pieces, a lot of time is spent practicing how to attack (and defend) from set pieces. A defending team, for example, will adopt positions and patterns of movement, such as the wall where the defending players stand in a line, to stop an easy goal.

Legendary free-kick

In 1997, Roberto Carlos (see below) scored from an incredible direct free-kick. He hit the ball so far to the right of the French wall that a ballboy between the corner flag and the goalpost ducked. Miraculously, the ball swerved in and landed in the goal. Carlos' "banana shot" has entered soccer folklore.

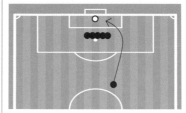

With a shot that seemed to defy the laws of physics, Carlos swerved the ball around the wall.

● Roberto Carlos (Brazil)
● Defending team (France)
— Trajectory of ball

> TEAMS **SPEND A LOT OF TIME** PRACTICING **HOW TO ATTACK** FROM SET PIECES.

ROBERTO CARLOS

Brazilian wingback Roberto Carlos is known for his trademark free-kicks. His seemingly impossible "banana shot" is legendary. He has played for the Brazil national team in three World Cup tournaments, helping them reach the final in 1998 and to win in 2002.

The offside rule

Offside is the most contentious and frequently misunderstood rule in soccer, as decisions often rest on an official's individual interpretation of the law. It is also the most frequently revised rule, as minor changes to the regulations can have dramatic effects on the character of matches.

What is the rule?

A player is ruled offside when the ball is passed forward by his teammates if: he's in the opponent's half of the field; he's closer to the opponent's goal line than the ball; there are less than two defenders closer to the goal line than himself. Only the head, body, and legs are considered. The player is onside if he's level with the second defender from the goal line or if he receives the ball from a throw-in, corner, or goal-kick.

KEY	
●	Attacking team
●	Defending team
○	Goalkeeper
---	Pass

OFFSIDE

In this situation, Player A is offside because there is only one defender—the goalkeeper (1)—between him and the goal line when Player B passes the ball. An indirect free-kick would be awarded for this offense.

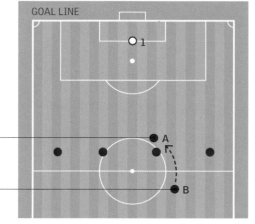

Player A is in an offside position

Player B passes the ball to Player A, who is offside

ONSIDE

Player A is not offside in this case. This is because when Player B passed the ball, there were two defenders between Player A and the goal line.

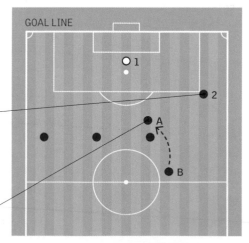

Both the goalkeeper (1) and another defender (2) are between Player A and the goal line

Player A is in an onside position

Offside or not?

The offside rule has many nuances that often make rulings very subjective. There are, for example, many situations in which a player is in an offside position but is not deemed to be violating the offside rule. The following scenarios illustrate some of the peculiarities of the rule.

KEY	
● Attacking team	---- Pass
● Defending team	— Player
○ Goalkeeper	movement

SCENARIO ONE

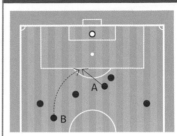

ONSIDE
Player A is in an offside position when he receives the ball but was onside when it was played forward by his teammate. Hence, he is onside.

SCENARIO TWO

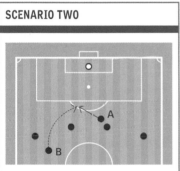

OFFSIDE
Player A, who is receiving the ball, was in an offside position when the ball was played forward by Player B. He is therefore offside.

SCENARIO THREE

ONSIDE
Player C on the left wing is in an offside position. However, as he is not interfering with play between Players A and B, he is deemed to be onside.

SCENARIO FOUR

OFFSIDE
Player A receives the ball in an onside position but was offside at the moment it was passed forward by Player B. So, Player A is offside.

SCENARIO FIVE

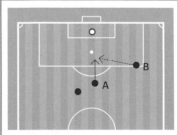

ONSIDE
Although Player A receives the ball in an offside position, he is actually onside because he was behind the ball at the moment that it was played.

Fouls and infringements

Since the FA's Laws of the Game (see pp.10–13) were first drawn up in 1863, many offenses have been written into the rulebook as fouls. Referees, equipped with red and yellow cards, have been employed to enforce them.

Crime and punishment

A foul is committed by a player when he has contravened Law 12 of the Laws of the Game. This includes kicking, tripping, or striking an opponent, connecting with a player before connecting with the ball when tackling, and deliberately handling the ball. Red and yellow cards are used to punish serious fouls, while free-kicks are awarded for lesser fouls.

Direct and indirect free-kicks

A direct free-kick is awarded to the opposing team when a player commits a dangerous or "penal" foul, such as charging at an opponent with excessive force or performing a high tackle. A goal may be scored directly from this type of free-kick (see pp.14–17). The opposing team is awarded an indirect free-kick when a player commits a foul other than a dangerous or penal foul, or infringes technical requirements. A goal cannot be scored directly from this type of free-kick (a second player must first touch the ball). See below and opposite for some typical fouls.

❝ IN ADDITION TO **AWARDING FREE-KICKS**, THE REFEREE CAN PENALIZE A PLAYER BY ISSUING HIM WITH EITHER A **YELLOW OR RED CARD**. **❞**

It is a foul for a player to use his body to block another player

High tackles are considered to be dangerous play

OBSTRUCTION
If a player is positioned between the ball and an opponent and makes no attempt to play the ball, it is known as obstruction.

HIGH TACKLE
Whether attempting to play the ball or not, tackles made with "high feet" have become less acceptable in soccer.

It is a foul to deliberately trip an opponent

It is a foul for a player to hold back an opponent

HOLDING

Pulling on a player's shirt to slow him down in an attempt to gain possession of the ball contravenes the Laws of the Game.

TRIPPING

Tripping has long been an offense, but the referee must be sharp-eyed to see if there really has been contact between the players.

A sliding tackle can be a serious offense if not executed properly

SLIDING TACKLE

A sliding tackle, in which the attacking player fails to gain possession of the ball, is considered to be a serious foul.

The card system

In addition to awarding free-kicks, the referee can penalize an individual player by issuing him with either a yellow or red card. A yellow card (or caution) is issued for serious offenses or dissent. A red card is issued for very serious or violent offenses and results in the player being sent off immediately. If a player receives two yellow cards in the same game, he will also be sent off.

YELLOW CARD OFFENSES
- Dissent by word or action
- Persistent infringement of the rules
- Delaying the restart of play, and deliberate time-wasting
- Making a poorly timed and dangerous tackle
- Entering or leaving the field without the referee's permission
- Unsportmanlike behavior

RED CARD OFFENSES
- Serious foul play
- Violent conduct, or using foul language
- Spitting at an opponent or other person
- Denying the opposing team a goal or potential chance at goal by deliberately handling the ball (except the goalkeeper inside his own penalty area)
- Receiving two cautions in one match

The officials

In professional matches, the game is controlled by four officials: the referee (see below and opposite), two assistant referees (see pp.24–25), and the fourth official (see p.26). The referee has full authority and, aided by the other officials, is tasked with enforcing the 17 Laws of the Game (see pp.10–13).

The referee's hand signals

Referees use various hand signals to indicate decisions to players. They also blow a whistle to stop play before making the signal. A short, quick whistle indicates a less serious offense, while more serious fouls elicit harder blasts.

YELLOW CARD
A yellow card is held up, above the head, to the player being cautioned.

RED CARD
A red card is held up, above the head, to the player being sent off.

DIRECT FREE-KICK
The referee blows the whistle and points in the direction of the kick.

INDIRECT FREE-KICK
A hand is held up until the taker and a teammate have touched the ball.

ADVANTAGE
The referee extends both arms to indicate that play can continue.

PENALTY-KICK
The referee points to the appropriate penalty mark.

GOAL-KICK
The referee points toward the appropriate part of the goal area.

CORNER-KICK
The referee points toward the appropriate corner arc.

Refereeing systems

Early matches were played without the referee on the field, but from the late 1890s it became clear that a coordinated and mobile approach to refereeing was needed. Several systems of patrolling the field have since been developed.

KEY	
<------>	Linear system
<------>	Diagonal system
<------>	Zigzag-path system

ASSISTANT REFEREE 1

ASSISTANT REFEREE

ASSISTANT REFEREE 2

LINEAR SYSTEM
The referee patrols one side of the field, while one or two assistants cover the opposite sideline. However, the referee may obstruct wing play.

DIAGONAL SYSTEM
The referee patrols a diagonal area between two opposing corner flags, while the assistant referees stand on opposite sides.

ZIGZAG-PATH SYSTEM
If the referee officiates alone, he may move in a steady zigzag path in a line between the two penalty arcs, changing positions for corners and penalty kicks.

" A SHORT, QUICK WHISTLE USUALLY INDICATES A LESS SERIOUS OFFENSE, WHILE MORE SERIOUS FOULS ELICIT HARDER BLASTS. "

REFEREE'S DUTIES
The match is controlled by the referee, who enforces the rules for the match to which he has been appointed. His main duties are:

ENFORCE THE RULES
The referee's main task is to enforce the rules set out in the Laws of the Game.

CONTROL THE MATCH
He must control the match with the assistant referees and, for official matches, the fourth official.

CHECK EQUIPMENT
He must ensure that the ball and the players' equipment meet the requirements as stated in the Laws of the Game.

TIMEKEEP AND MAINTAIN RECORDS
The referee must act as the timekeeper for the match, and keep a record of any substitutions and offenses.

STOP PLAY WHEN NECESSARY
It is the duty of the referee to stop, suspend, or abandon the match in case there are any infringements of the Laws of the Game, or because of any other outside interference.

ENSURE PLAYER SAFETY
He must stop the match if a player is seriously injured, and ensure that he is removed from the field of play.

Assistant referee

The assistant referee helps the referee to officiate a match. In professional games, two assistants patrol each sideline. They each take responsibility for one half of the field, diagonally opposing each other (see "Refereeing systems," p.23). They officiate in situations in which the referee is not in a position to make the best decision. Although crucial, their role is purely advisory.

The role of assistants

The more senior of the two assistants usually oversees the side of the field that contains the technical areas, so that he can help supervise substitutions. Typical duties for assistants include signaling for offside and determining which team should be awarded a throw-in.

> ❝ THE **ASSISTANT REFEREE** INDICATES WHICH SIDE IS **ENTITLED TO A GOAL-KICK, CORNER-KICK, OR THROW-IN**. ❞

ASSISTANT REFEREE'S DUTIES

The assistant referee assists with refereeing decisions. His or her duties include:

SIGNALING FOR OUT OF PLAY

The assistant referee signals when the ball leaves the field of play.

SIGNALING FOR RESTARTS

The assistant indicates which side is entitled to a goal-kick, corner-kick, or throw-in.

SIGNALING FOR OFFSIDE

The assistant referee signals when a player is in an offside position.

SIGNALING FOR SUBSTITUTIONS

He or she signals when a substitution has been requested.

SIGNALING FOR MISCONDUCT

The assistant signals when misconduct occurs out of the referee's field of vision.

MONITORING THE GOALKEEPER

He or she monitors the goalkeeper during penalty-kicks, signaling if he moves off his line before the kick.

THE GENDER AGENDA

The role of "linesman" was added to the Laws of the Game (see pp.10–13) in 1891—at a time when the officials were always male. It wasn't until 1996 that the term was dropped in favor of the gender-neutral "assistant referee."

Flag signals

The flag is the assistant's most important piece of equipment, as flag signals are the standard form of communication with a referee (although a buzzer system is sometimes also used). The distinctive red and yellow checkered design of the flag has been proven to be the most eye-catching color combination over a long distance. The following signals are most commonly used during a match.

OFFSIDE
The flag is held above the head to signal for an offside offense.

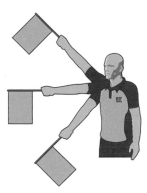

OFFSIDE POSITION
A high flag is for far offside, a horizontal flag for middle, and a low flag for near offside.

SUBSTITUTION
A flag is held above the head with both hands to indicate a substitution.

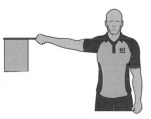

THROW-IN
A flag is held out to one side, pointing in the direction of play of the team awarded the throw.

Other signals

In addition to using flag signals and a buzzer system, assistant referees employ a variety of other forms of communication. Discrete hand signals, for example, indicate that a close ball has not gone out of play or that no offense has been committed. In return, the referee can use hand signals to inform an assistant the direction in which a throw-in should be taken if he or she is unsure.

CALLING TIME
A clenched fist on the chest means 45 minutes have elapsed in the half.

NO OFFENSE
The assistant referee shows a lowered palm to indicate that no offense has been committed.

Fourth official

The fourth official assists the referee with administrative duties before and after the game, helps with assessing players' equipment, and may be called on to replace another match official (see below). He also sets and holds up electronic display boards, acts as another pair of eyes for the referee, and keeps an extra set of records.

The fourth official as substitute

The fourth official may replace the assistant referee or the referee. If an assistant is injured, for example, the fourth official replaces him automatically. If a referee cannot continue, the fourth official may replace him directly, or an assistant may replace the referee, with the fourth official taking the assistant's position.

> THE **FOURTH OFFICIAL** KEEPS A **DUPLICATE SET OF RECORDS** AND ACTS AS AN **EXTRA PAIR OF EYES** FOR THE REFEREE.

FOURTH OFFICIAL'S DUTIES
The fourth official has the following duties:

ASSISTING WITH RECORD KEEPING
The fourth official keeps a duplicate set of records.

CHECKING PLAYERS' EQUIPMENT
He helps the referee check that the players' equipment meets the requirements set out in the rules.

OVERSEEING SUBSTITUTIONS
He ensures that substitutions are conducted in an orderly manner.

DISPLAYING INFORMATION
He uses numbered boards or electronic displays to inform the referee of any substitution, and to show the amount of time added at the end of each half.

MAINTAINING CONTROL
He maintains control in the teams' technical areas, intervening when coaches, bench personnel, or substitutes become argumentative.

ACTING AS AN INTERMEDIARY
He is the contact point between the match officials and non-participants, such as stadium managers, broadcast crews, and ball retrievers.

uefa·com

SUPPORTING ROLE

Among other duties, the fourth official holds up a display board to indicate any time added on at the end of each half (advised by the referee).

Officials' equipment

The referee and the assistant referees make use of several different pieces of equipment. These are all designed to help the referee enforce the Laws of the Game (see pp.10–13) effectively.

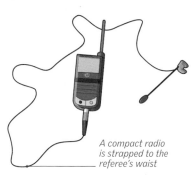

A compact radio is strapped to the referee's waist

EARPIECE AND RADIO SET
In all top-flight matches, referees and their assistants communicate by using a small radio set.

ASSISTANT'S FLAGS
Flags are used by the assistant referees to signal to the referee (see p.25 for assistant's signals).

TIMEPIECE
The referee must have at least one timepiece—such as a wrist watch and a stopwatch.

CARDS AND NOTEBOOK
The referee may decide to penalize players by issuing yellow or red cards. Incidents are recorded in a notebook.

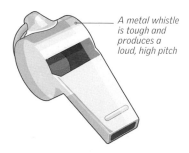

A metal whistle is tough and produces a loud, high pitch

WHISTLE
The referee blows his whistle to start play, stop or delay play due to a foul or injury, and to end each half.

A built-in needle fits directly into the valve of the ball

PRESSURE GAUGE
A pressure gauge is used by the referee to check that the ball has been correctly inflated.

Shirts, shorts, and socks

For official games, it is compulsory for players to wear a shirt or jersey, shorts, socks, shoes or cleats (see pp.30–31), and shin pads (see p.32). All the players on a team (except for the goalkeeper) must wear matching uniforms. While shirts may feature stripes or patterned designs, shorts are usually one color.

Referee's decision
A player who is not wearing the correct uniform will be asked to leave the field by the referee and may only return when the referee confirms that his uniform is correct.

A shirt made from modern synthetic material absorbs water corresponding to only 0.4 percent of its weight (the comparable figure for cotton is 7 percent)

Shorts are also made of similar synthetic material and are usually simpler in design

An elastane content "molds" the sock to the body, while padded foot-beds ensure comfort

Shirts

Modern soccer shirts, made of durable synthetic material, help carry air and moisture away from the body, while retaining warmth when needed. Reversed seams prevent rubbing and soreness, and undershirts help increase comfort and aid ventilation.

Shorts

Modern shorts are loose, which allows for freedom of movement and good air circulation. These shorts are considerably longer than they were in 1960s and '70s.

Socks

Socks are an integral part of a soccer player's uniform and must entirely cover the shin pad.

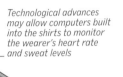

Technological advances may allow computers built into the shirts to monitor the wearer's heart rate and sweat levels

❝ A PLAYER WHO IS NOT WEARING THE CORRECT UNIFORM MAY BE ASKED TO LEAVE THE PITCH. ❞

BREATHABLE MATERIAL

Tiny pores in the fabric let air reach the player's body, while allowing the release of moisture from the skin. The pores are too small for raindrops to penetrate.

HOME AND AWAY

The first clash of uniforms in the world came in 1890, when Sunderland played Wolverhampton Wanderers (both teams wore red and white stripes at the time). Sunderland was the home team and, in accordance with the rules of the English league, was required to change uniform. In 1921, however, the rules were reversed, with the away team required to change (although both teams had to change in FA Cup games played at a neutral ground).

GOALKEEPER'S SHIRT

As the only player who is allowed to handle the ball, it is important that the goalkeeper is easily identifiable. For this reason, in 1909, goalkeepers could wear white, scarlet, or blue shirts. In 1912, the green shirt was introduced as an option. In the 1970s, regulations were relaxed, allowing manufacturers to experiment with designs.

SHIRT NUMBERS

Shirt numbers were first used in 1928 to help referees and the crowd identify players. They corresponded to fixed playing positions, with the center forward (see p.53), for example, always allocated the number nine. As formations have evolved, however, this practice has become rare. Today, "squad" numbers are used, with individual players being designated a number for the whole season.

Shoes

Players need comfortable, lightweight, and durable footwear that grips the playing surface. The soccer shoe should be flexible enough to maximize performance but sturdy enough to reduce the risk of injury. On grass, players wear cleats (see opposite for types of cleats); on artificial turf, players wear athletic shoes with rubber studs on the sole.

Modern soccer shoes

Modern shoes are extremely light and flexible, and are made from an array of synthetic fabrics and plastics. Kangaroo leather, which is markedly stronger, lighter, and more supple than other leathers, is widely used in shoe manufacture.

> ON ARTIFICIAL TURF, PLAYERS WEAR **ATHLETIC SHOES WITH RUBBER STUDS** ON THE SOLE.

An outer coating on some shoes increases the level of friction for kicking

The insoles can be premolded to the player's feet for a perfect fit

An elasticated tongue covers the shoelaces for a larger kicking area

Synthetic materials reduce water absorption, which helps keep the shoe light

TECHNOLOGICAL DEVELOPMENTS

While innovations in modern soccer shoe design may appear to be limited to a profusion of often garish colors and logos, there have, in fact, been a number of significant technological developments. These have had wide-ranging implications for performance and play.

A molded, reinforced heel stiffener supports the heel and protects against injuries

SCREW-IN CLEATS
Detachable cleats are used for wet conditions. Different lengths can be used.

FIXED CLEATS
Shoes with fixed or "molded" cleats are used for standard turf conditions.

BLADED STUDS
Shoes with fixed "blades" provide a stable base on firm natural turf that is too hard for cleats.

SOLE BRIDGE
A microfiber bridge links the cleats at the front and the back of the shoe. This provides stability and flexibility.

Protective gear

Gear meant to protect players during play is an important part of their uniform. Shin pads, which are made from plastic, are worn to protect the shins, and must be covered entirely by socks. Goalkeepers can wear protective headgear and gloves that provide grip and hand protection when catching the ball.

High-impact and anatomically designed outer shell protects the shin

Shin pads

Shin pads are made from plastic polymers and fiberglass. They are strapped to the shin, under the sock, and help prevent fractures to the tibia resulting from rough tackles. Pads were made compulsory by FIFA in 1990.

Soccer headgear is flexible but tough enough to prevent injuries

M100

SHINGUARD

Headgear

Protective headgear is designed to cushion the head from collisions with other players, the ground, or the goalposts. It is almost always worn by the goalkeepers.

" GLOVES ARE NOW UNIVERSALLY WORN BY GOALKEEPERS TO INCREASE GRIP ON THE BALL AND PROTECT THE HANDS. "

Goalkeeper's gloves

All players may wear gloves, although up until the 1970s, few chose to do so. Gloves are now universally worn by goalkeepers to increase grip on the ball and protect the hands. They are made from strong synthetic materials and are segmented to aid flexibility. Protectors prevent the fingers from bending backward.

Velcro straps secure the pad tightly to the leg

MILA MOMA

M100

MILA MOMA

PALM PROTECTION
The palm area of the glove is made from materials designed to enhance grip and protection.

The ball

Modern soccer balls consist of an outer covering of synthetic leather panels stitched together to form a spherical surface. Real leather, which was used until the 1980s, often absorbed water, making the ball heavy. Inside the outer layer is the air bladder, which is usually made from latex or butyl. Between the bladder and the outer cover is an inner lining, which gives the ball its bounce.

FIFA requirements

According to the Laws of the Game (see pp.10–13), the ball must be spherical, made from leather or other suitable materials, and have a circumference of 27–28in (68.5–71cm). At the start of the match, the ball should weigh $14^1/_2$–16oz (410–450g) and be inflated to a pressure of $8^1/_2$–$15^1/_2$lb/sq in (600–1,100g/sq cm). These requirements were set in 1872 and have remained largely unchanged ever since.

SOCCER BALL CONSTRUCTION

There are four main components of a ball: the outer cover, the stitching, the inner lining, and the bladder. The quality of materials used for them can affect how the ball behaves.

Panels on professional balls are stitched together by hand using polyester thread to form a tight, strong seam

Laboratory testing

A ball's level of bounce, ability to swerve through the air, level of air-retention, and overall longevity can all be altered by its design. Recent developments in the use of synthetic materials and production techniques have produced balls that maximize the transfer of energy from the kicker to the ball and are flight-accurate. FIFA-approved balls are all laboratory-tested for balance, bounce, shape, trajectory, velocity, and water absorption.

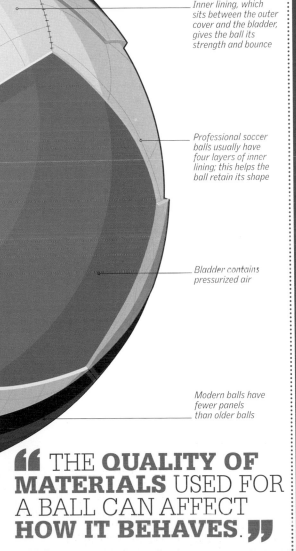

Modern covers are made from synthetic leathers such as polyurethane (PU) and polyvinyl chloride (PVC)

THE VALVE
In professional soccer balls, the valve is silicone-treated to prevent air loss and to aid the smooth insertion of the inflating needle.

Inner lining, which sits between the outer cover and the bladder, gives the ball its strength and bounce

Professional soccer balls usually have four layers of inner lining; this helps the ball retain its shape

Bladder contains pressurized air

Modern balls have fewer panels than older balls

❝ THE QUALITY OF MATERIALS USED FOR A BALL CAN AFFECT HOW IT BEHAVES. ❞

The goal

Soccer would be nothing without goals, so great importance is placed on the design of these structures. They must be safe and reliable, and must not obscure the spectators' view. They also need to be durable. Nets, for example, used to be made of string and had to be taken down between matches to prevent them from rotting. Today, they are made from weatherproof synthetic fibers.

Goal requirements

The Laws of the Game (see pp.10–13) state that a goal must be placed on the center of each goal line and consist of two upright posts joined at the top by a crossbar. It should be equidistant from the corner flagposts and may be made of wood, metal, or other approved material. The posts and crossbar must be white. The goal must be securely anchored.

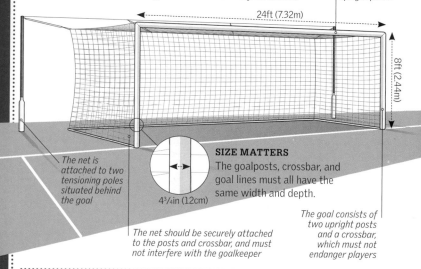

The crossbar must be the same width and color as the upright posts

24ft (7.32m)

8ft (2.44m)

The net is attached to two tensioning poles situated behind the goal

4³⁄₄in (12cm)

SIZE MATTERS
The goalposts, crossbar, and goal lines must all have the same width and depth.

The net should be securely attached to the posts and crossbar, and must not interfere with the goalkeeper

The goal consists of two upright posts and a crossbar, which must not endanger players

How the net is hung

There are several net-hanging systems. The two main considerations for their design are: the tension of the net should be such that it is clear when a goal is scored; and the ball should not rebound off or become lodged in the back stanchion.

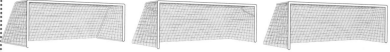

BALL-AND-SOCKET SYSTEM
In the 1970s, net extensions were plugged into sockets that screwed into posts and crossbar.

EXTRUSION SYSTEM
In the 1980s, triangular brackets projecting back from corners of the goal helped tighten the net.

NET-TENSIONING SYSTEM
In the 1990s, goal nets were clipped onto fixed aluminum mounts that worked like curtain rods.

Different goal sizes

The dimensions of the goal vary depending on the type of soccer being played. In five-a-side, for example, the ball must not go above head height, so the goal is low. In beach soccer, the goal is slightly smaller than it is for professional matches, because the sand makes it difficult for the goalkeeper to cover distances quickly.

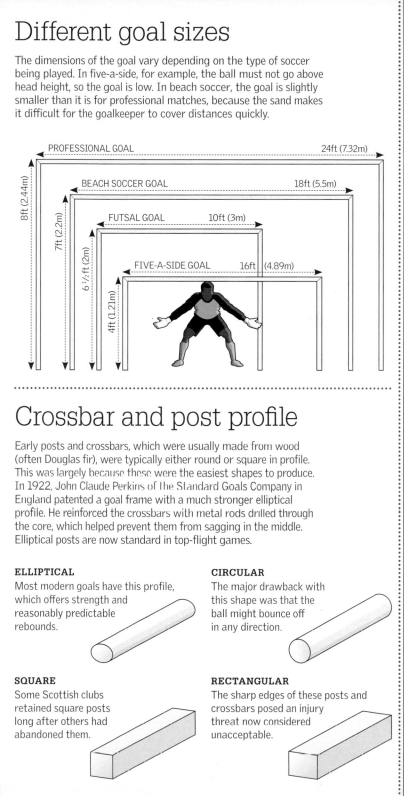

PROFESSIONAL GOAL — 24ft (7.32m)
8ft (2.44m)

BEACH SOCCER GOAL — 18ft (5.5m)
7ft (2.2m)

FUTSAL GOAL — 10ft (3m)
6½ft (2m)

FIVE-A-SIDE GOAL — 16ft (4.89m)
4ft (1.21m)

Crossbar and post profile

Early posts and crossbars, which were usually made from wood (often Douglas fir), were typically either round or square in profile. This was largely because these were the easiest shapes to produce. In 1922, John Claude Perkins of the Standard Goals Company in England patented a goal frame with a much stronger elliptical profile. He reinforced the crossbars with metal rods drilled through the core, which helped prevent them from sagging in the middle. Elliptical posts are now standard in top-flight games.

ELLIPTICAL
Most modern goals have this profile, which offers strength and reasonably predictable rebounds.

CIRCULAR
The major drawback with this shape was that the ball might bounce off in any direction.

SQUARE
Some Scottish clubs retained square posts long after others had abandoned them.

RECTANGULAR
The sharp edges of these posts and crossbars posed an injury threat now considered unacceptable.

The field

Professional soccer is played on a flat grass or
artificial turf field, with set markings. The area
of the field may vary. The playing area must be
rectangular—the length of the sideline must
be greater than the length of the goal line.

The field of play
The outer extremes of the field are
delineated by the sidelines and goal
lines: if the ball wholly crosses the
sideline it is out of play; if it crosses
the goal line between the goal
posts a goal is scored. If part
of the ball is on the line,
it is still in play.

Technical area
*One person at a
time can instruct
from this 3ft (1m)
area that extends
on either side of
the dugout*

18yd (16.5m)

49–98yd (45–90m)

12yd (11m)

10yd (9.15m)

10yd (9.15m)

6yd (5.5m)

6yd (5.5m)

10yd (9.15m)

12cm (4¾in)

Penalty spot
*The penalty spot is 12yd (11m)
from the goal line. Penalty
kicks are taken from here*

Goal area
*Also known as the six-yard
box, goal kicks are taken from
anywhere inside this area*

Penalty area
*The goalkeeper can handle
the ball anywhere inside
this 18-yard box. Fouls
committed in this area
result in a penalty kick*

Center mark and circle
*A game begins, or
restarts after a goal
or following half time,
from the center mark*

❝ OPPOSING
PLAYERS MUST
**NOT ENCROACH
INSIDE THE
CENTER CIRCLE**
UNTIL THE KICK-
OFF HAS TAKEN
PLACE. ❞

IMPERFECT FIELD?

English team Yeovil Town's former field
at Huish was renowned in the game for
its alarmingly sloping field. There was
a difference in height of approximately
6ft (1.8m) from one side of the field to
the other. The site of the old field is now
home to a supermarket.

> **THE OUTER EXTREMES OF THE FIELD ARE DELINEATED BY THE SIDELINES AND GOAL LINES.**

Goal
A goal is placed in the center of each goal line and must be 8yd (7.32m) long

Goal line
When the ball crosses this line, a goal kick or corner is awarded, depending on which team kicked it out

Corner arc
Corner kicks are taken from the corner arc, which has a radius of 1yd (1m)

18yd (16.5m)

8yd (7.32m)

98–131yd (90–120m)

Halfway line
This line divides the playing area into two

Sideline
If the ball crosses this line, a throw-in is awarded to the team that didn't put the ball out of play

SIZE MATTERS

Barcelona's Nou Camp stadium has one of the largest fields in the world. It measures 115yd x 78yd (105m x 72m). Opened in 1957, the stadium has a capacity of nearly 99,000.

Field dimension

The position of the field markings is unchangeable, although there is a degree of flexibility regarding the length of these lines. Field sizes vary depending on whether matches are being played in domestic or international competitions.

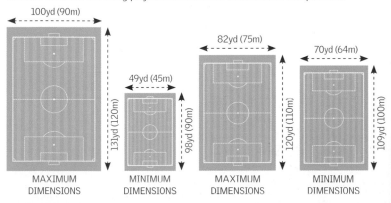

100yd (90m)

49yd (45m)

131yd (120m)

98yd (90m)

MAXIMUM DIMENSIONS

MINIMUM DIMENSIONS

82yd (75m)

70yd (64m)

120yd (110m)

109yd (100m)

MAXIMUM DIMENSIONS

MINIMUM DIMENSIONS

DOMESTIC GAMES
The size of the field can range between the measurements shown above, as long as the field does not become square.

INTERNATIONAL GAMES
Field dimensions can vary within allowed parameters, although the range is narrower than it is for domestic matches.

Player Positions

Goalkeepers

The goalkeeper is the last line of defense between the attacking players and the goal. The outcome of a match can often depend more on the goalkeeper than any other player. Each team must have a goalkeeper on the field at all times. If he is injured or is sent off, a substitute must be used. If no substitutes are available, another outfield player must assume the role.

The goalkeeper's role

Goalkeeping requires courage, quick reactions, and good concentration. Within his own penalty area, the goalkeeper can use any part of his body to control the ball—including the hands. He must defend his team's goal, prevent the opposition from scoring, and organize the defenders.

Essential skills

A goalkeeper essentially has to save, clear, marshall the defense, and distribute the ball. In addition to being a "safe pair of hands," he must show strength of character. If an outfield player makes a mistake, for example, a teammate may be able to salvage the situation; if a goalkeeper errs, the consequences are usually a confidence-shattering goal. Therefore, he must be strong enough to deal with any flack.

Quick reactions and a willingness to dive are important skills for the goalkeeper

A well-placed punch will clear the ball away

SAVING
Keeping the ball out of the net is the goalkeeper's main job. He must stop and block any shots at goal and use his height well to pluck high crosses out of the air.

CLEARING
Goalkeepers need to get the ball away from danger areas quickly, whether with their feet or via a punch, making sure the ball doesn't go back to the opposition.

RENÉ HIGUITA

Colombian goalkeeper René Higuita is famous for his "scorpion kick" (pictured). During a friendly match at Wembley in 1995, Higuita allowed the lobbed ball to float over his head before turning himself into a human scorpion and kicking it back into play with his heels.

> THE **OUTCOME OF A MATCH OFTEN DEPENDS** MORE ON THE **GOALKEEPER** THAN ANY OTHER PLAYER.

The goalkeeper is instrumental in organizing the defense and relaying advice

The keeper quickly decides which player is best placed to receive the ball

MARSHALING

Goalkeepers are in charge of the goal area and must organize their defenders. This is particularly important during free-kicks, when the goalkeeper organizes the wall.

DISTRIBUTION

Once the ball is safely in the goalkeeper's hands, he looks to find an available teammate and punts or throws the ball to him as quickly as possible.

Defenders

Defenders are responsible for preventing the attacking team from scoring and for winning back possession of the ball so that a counter-attack can be mounted. They can be categorized as either "central" (see opposite) or "wide" (see p.46). The defender must force the attacking team to make mistakes by marking opponents closely, intercepting their passes, and gaining possession of the ball.

Skills required

The defender must be a highly skilled player who is able to bring the ball out of defense in a controlled way before making accurate passes to teammates who are better placed to set up attacking moves. An ability to accurately anticipate threats is important, as is possessing the necessary levels of concentration to focus on the task in hand. He needs courage and excellent technical ability to make last-ditch tackles in front of the goal mouth. Strength and precision will also enable him to deal effectively with one-on-one attacks wherever they occur on the field.

The player being marked is under constant pressure from the defender

MARKING

When a defender shadows an attacker, this is known as marking. The defender may be able to intercept the ball or dissuade an attacker from passing to a marked teammate.

Defenders need fast reflexes to intercept well

INTERCEPTING

When a defender intercepts an attacker's pass, this is often the result of the pressure applied by the defending team as a whole, through persistent marking and closing down available space.

You will launch a feet-first slide toward the ball; he must take the ball and not the player

TACKLING

Using the feet to take the ball away from a player is known as tackling. The sliding tackle (shown above) is very effective, but the defender's timing must be perfect. There is also a risk of conceding a foul.

Central defenders

The role of central defender, which includes the positions center back and sweeper (see below), requires constant alertness and great physical strength. The ability to anticipate danger before it materializes—and take effective preventative action—is often fundamental to a team's success.

Center back

The center back is a team's last line of defense. He should have the ability to tackle effectively and win the ball. The center back needs to be tall, especially so that he can win the ball when it is in the air. He should also be powerful, fearless, decisive, and willing to make all-or-nothing tackles.

The sweeper

As the name suggests, the role of the sweeper is to "sweep up" the ball if the attacking team breaks through the defensive line. He does not mark a specific attacker, remaining "fluid", and is free to roam around the goal mouth, closing down any gaps in defense.

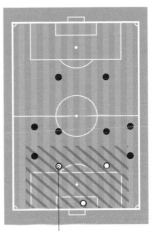

The center backs are responsible for patrolling the area in front of the goal mouth

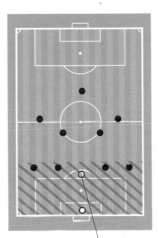

The sweeper roams laterally in front of the goal, but can advance upfield

CENTER BACK'S DOMAIN

A team typically places two center backs in front of the goalkeeper. They mark the most advanced attacking forward, aiming to bring the ball away from the penalty area.

THE SWEEPER'S DOMAIN

The sweeper is usually positioned behind the center backs. As he has no marking duties, he may travel a long way forward when his team is in possession.

❝ THE ROLE OF A CENTRAL DEFENDER REQUIRES CONSTANT ALERTNESS AND PHYSICAL STRENGTH. ❞

Wide defenders

The standard four-man defense consists of two center backs
(see p.45) in the middle of the field and two fullbacks to the side.
A further wide defender, the wingback, will regularly advance a long
way down the flanks. All wide defenders are expected to prevent the
opposing team from launching attacks down the flanks, and to join in
with their own team's attacks.

Fullback

The fullback has to stay wide and
prevent the attacking team from
developing attacks down the flanks.
He must be quick, and will usually
mark a designated forward. He should
also join in with attacking play.

Wingback

The wingback is a cross between the
fullback and the winger (see p.50). He
must defend like a fullback, preventing
attackers from reaching the goal line,
while charging forward like a winger
when his team is in possession.

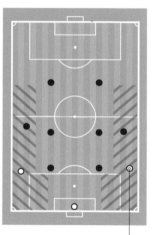

*One of the fullbacks
may advance up the
field during attacks*

*The wingback
ranges up
the field*

FULLBACK'S DOMAIN
The fullback operates on either the
right- or left-hand side of the field and
defends the flanks. When one fullback
goes on a forward run, the other "tucks
in" to support the central defenders.

WINGBACK'S DOMAIN
The wingback operates on either
the right- or left-hand side of the field,
but farther upfield than the fullback.
He is responsible for both defending
and attacking along the flanks.

STAR DEFENDERS: BEST BACK FOURS
Successful teams are invariably built
on solid defenses. The following back
fours provided the greatest defensive
support in the history of the game.

BRAZIL (1958)
While center backs Hilderado Bellini and
Orlando, and fullbacks Nilton Santos and
Djalma Santos may not have invented

the phenomenon of the "back four,"
they were the first to perfect it. This
formidable unit helped propel Brazil
to victory at the 1958 World Cup.

LEEDS UNITED (1960s–70s)
Jack Charlton, Norman Hunter, Terry
Cooper, and Paul Reaney didn't exactly
have a delicate touch when it came to
tackling, but they were highly effective.

The "back four"

The members of a standard four-man defense are known as the "back four." This unit consists of two fullbacks (see opposite) and two center backs (see p.45), or two fullbacks, one center back, and one sweeper (see p.45). The back four work together as a coordinated unit providing defensive cover across the whole width of the field.

CARLES PUYOL

Spanish defender Carles Puyol was awarded the "Best European Rightback" award by UEFA in 2002.

> **"** THE MEMBERS OF A **STANDARD FOUR-MAN DEFENSE** ARE KNOWN AS THE **'BACK FOUR.' "**

Back four as a unit

Good attacking begins with a solid defense. A strong back four should be well organized, committed, and focused. The unit must contain a mix of talented players who are able to work together to wrong-foot the attacking team. At the highest level of the game, the pressure to perform can be immense—especially given that an attacker who outwits the back four will almost certainly score.

The Leeds team of the late 1960s and early '70s owed much of its success to this hard-as-nails back four.

AC MILAN (1980s–90s)
Sweeper Franco Baresi, center back Alessandro Costacurta, and fullbacks Mauro Tassotti and Paolo Maldini formed one of the greatest back four defense units of all time at AC Milan during the 1980s and '90s. They won three European Cup and Champions League titles.

AFC AJAX (1995)
Center backs Frank Rijkaard and Danny Blind, and fullbacks Frank de Boer and Michael Reizeger were the Amsterdam team's formidable back four in the Champions League winning side of 1995.

Midfielders

As the name implies, midfielders play in the middle of the field between the defenders (see pp.44–47) and the forwards (see pp.52–57). Depending on the formation being used (see pp.142–49), there can be three, four, or five in a team. Their precise roles vary accordingly, but they can be categorized as "central" or "wide." They have to anticipate and exploit as many attacking opportunities as possible, as well as be actively involved in both defense and attack.

Skills required

Setting up goal-scoring opportunities is a major part of a midfielder's job. He must have excellent fitness, since he is required to cover the whole field, alternating between defense and attack as play dictates. To defend well, the midfielder needs to be an excellent tackler and be able to win aerial battles in the center of the field. In an attacking role, he has to be adept at tackling, passing, dribbling, and shooting.

A well-timed sliding tackle is an effective way to gain the ball

TACKLING

As part of his defensive duties, the midfielder must be an accomplished tackler. Much of the technique in tackling comes from pressuring the opponent before seizing the ball.

The midfielder must be equally at home making both short and long passes

Dribbling is the main way for a wide midfielder to move upfield

PASSING

The midfielder passes the ball around more often than other players on the field. Top-class performers may make 50 or more passes during a match, with a success rate above 80 percent.

DRIBBLING

The wide midfielder in particular needs good dribbling skills in order to get himself into positions from which he can deliver effective crosses into the opponent's penalty area.

Central midfielder—box-to-box

The central midfielder, as typified by the box-to-box midfielder, is the hardest-working player on the field. Technical skills such as dribbling and passing must become second nature, so that he can distribute the ball effectively to teammates. When he is not setting up offensive attacks or engineering plays, he drops back into defense to pressurize the attacking team.

Archetypal midfielder

The box-to-box player is the archetypal midfielder. He is actively involved in every part of the game, running from one penalty area to the other in an attempt to dominate play. He typically has incredible stamina and impeccable technical ability.

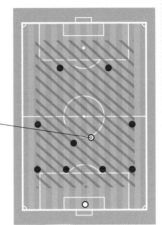

The box-to-box midfielder races from one end of the field to the other

BOX-TO-BOX PLAYER'S DOMAIN
The box-to-box midfielder covers the whole length of the center of the field. When on the offensive, he races up to the opposition's penalty area; when on the defensive, he races back to his own penalty area.

Central midfielder—holding

Primarily a defensive role, the holding midfielder is stationed between the other midfielders and the full- and wingbacks (see p.46). He is responsible for repelling attacking players who have made it through the midfield.

HOLDING MIDFIELDER'S DOMAIN
The holding midfielder operates farther back down the field than the box-to-box midfielder. He "holds back" attacking players by intercepting passes with hard tackling and shrewd positioning.

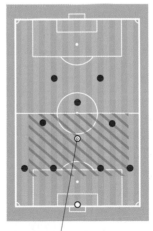

Holding midfielder has to prevent the attacking team from reaching the defenders

❝ SETTING UP **GOALSCORING OPPORTUNITIES** IS A MAJOR PART OF **A MIDFIELDER'S JOB**. HE MUST HAVE EXCELLENT FITNESS AS HE IS **REQUIRED TO COVER THE WHOLE FIELD**. **❞**

Central midfielder—playmaker

The playmaker is a midfielder who sets up attacking plays for the forwards (see pp.52–57), usually from a central position. He must have great passing ability and vision. A playmaker can either be "advanced" or "withdrawn" (see below).

Advanced playmaker

The advanced playmaker makes himself available for passes and can turn defensive moves into attacking ones by using short, incisive passes. He usually has to make passes in very little spaces.

Withdrawn playmaker

The withdrawn playmaker usually plays alongside a holding midfielder (see p.49). He takes advantage of the holding midfielder's support to launch long, decisive passes.

The advanced playmaker sets up attacks from the hole

The withdrawn playmaker sets up attacks from farther down the field

ADVANCED PLAYMAKER'S DOMAIN

The advanced playmaker plays in the "hole"—an area between midfield and the opposing line of defense. In occupying this position, he is hard for the attacking team to mark.

WITHDRAWN PLAYMAKER'S DOMAIN

Despite being relatively deep-lying, the withdrawn playmaker must set up attacks. He makes long balls either through the middle or to a wide player.

> ❝ **PLAYMAKERS SET UP ATTACKING PLAYS** FOR THE FORWARDS USUALLY FROM A **CENTRAL POSITION**. ❞

TRADITIONAL WINGERS

Prior to the mid-1960s, wingers were attacking players who rarely helped with defense. Stationed toward the sideline, they stretched the attacking team's defense and provided an outlet for their own defenders. Their main duty was to take the ball past the attacking team's fullback and deliver crosses into the penalty area. England's Stanley Matthews (1915–2000) was one of the all-time greats.

Central midfielder—attacking

A player with particularly attacking instincts often deployed relatively far upfield, the attacking central midfielder often produces excellent shots and contributes several goals during a season. He must have great vision and technical ability, including faultless passing and shooting skills.

Attacking central midfielders usually play upfield

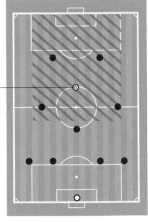

ATTACKING CENTRAL MIDFIELDER'S DOMAIN
With a talent for bursting into the attacking team's penalty area at exactly the right moment (either with or without the ball), the attacking central midfielder is positioned in an advanced position. He often forms the front point of a four-man diamond in a 4-4-2 formation (see p.145).

Wide midfielders

The wide midfielder is an attacking midfielder who focuses on one side of the field. He is relatively flexible in his movements rather than just sticking to the flanks. In recent years, his role has become very fluid. The rise of the wingback (see p.46) requires the modern winger to provide defensive cover when the wingback is upfield.

The modern wide midfielder stays wide to stretch the attacking team's defense

MODERN WIDE MIDFIELDER'S DOMAIN
Active in both defense and offense, the modern wide midfielder provides defensive cover by tracking back and moving in toward the middle to help maintain a tight defensive unit.

LIONEL MESSI

Lionel Messi is most effective when playing wide on the right. He can "cut in" with his stronger left foot before shooting, passing to a defender, or running with the ball.

Forwards

Forwards, or strikers, are positioned farthest forward on a team, nearest to the opponent's goal. They all have one essential job: to score goals. As well as taking advantage of goal-scoring opportunities, forwards are also expected to set up goals for other team players.

Skills required

Forwards must have pace (at least over short distances), show great courage, and have an instinctive eye for goal. Excellent shooting ability is a prerequisite, but heading, crossing, and passing skills are also vital for engineering goal-scoring opportunities and out-maneuvering defenders.

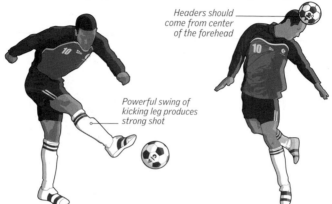

Headers should come from center of the forehead

Powerful swing of kicking leg produces strong shot

SHOOTING

There are many shooting techniques. However, the most common is a low, hard shot struck off the cleat's instep.

HEADING

Used for passing, shooting, or controlling the ball, heading is a versatile skill. It allows the player to reach high balls.

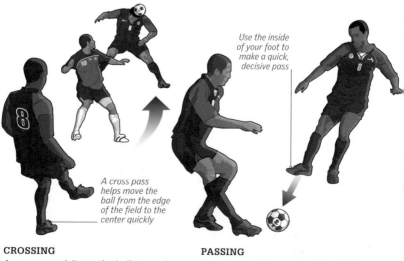

A cross pass helps move the ball from the edge of the field to the center quickly

Use the inside of your foot to make a quick, decisive pass

CROSSING

A cross pass delivers the ball toward players in attacking positions. Well-hit crosses are hard to defend against.

PASSING

A well-executed pass consists of three elements: the correct amount of power, appropriate direction, and good timing.

Center forward

With the aim of scoring as many goals as possible, the center forward is a tall, powerful player who fights his way to the ball before his opponents. Also known as a "target man," he usually operates near the goal, where he waits to "receive" the ball from teammates. He often scores from corners and crosses, using his height and strength to head the ball, or shield it from other players while they turn and shoot.

Skills required

The center forward must have superior strength and excellent heading ability. He must be an accurate shooter. Since he often plays with his back to the goal, he must have necessary ball control to retain possession of the ball while waiting for other players to enter the game and provide support.

Center forwards wait near the goal and act as focal points for attacks

> **A CENTER FORWARD, MUST BE AN ACCURATE SHOOTER WITH SUPERIOR STRENGTH AND EXCELLENT HEADING ABILITY.**

CENTER FORWARD'S DOMAIN

The center forward ranges up the field, focusing on the area in front of the opponent's goal. From here he is in the best position to receive balls, turn, and score.

ALAN SHEARER

Alan Shearer, who celebrated goals with a simple flat-palmed raise of the arm, scored a hat-trick on his full league debut for Southampton in 1988 and never looked back. He is living proof that old-style center forwards still have a place.

Withdrawn striker

The withdrawn striker has a similar role to the advanced playmaker midfielder (see p.50) in that he plays between the midfield and the opponent's defense, aiming to set up attacks. However, the withdrawn striker typically has just one player from his team in front of him, while advanced playmakers have two. Many of the greatest players in the game's history have been withdrawn strikers.

Room to roam

Exceptionally talented players, such as Diego Maradona and Zinédine Zidane, flourished in this position because it allowed them the freedom to roam the field and express creative instincts. In this position, the withdrawn striker must be aware of the positions of both teammates and opponents, and be able to instinctively time his runs so that players can pass to him. He must be an excellent passer of the ball, and be able to turn quickly and accelerate.

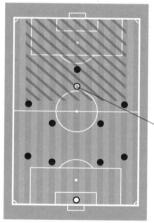

The withdrawn striker retains possession, sets up attacks, or shoots, from his position in the "hole"

WITHDRAWN STRIKER'S DOMAIN

The withdrawn striker exploits the space between the midfield and the opponent's defense (the "hole"). He holds up the ball, passes, and shoots.

GIANFRANCO ZOLA

Gianfranco Zola spent his formative years as an understudy to Diego Maradona at Napoli. In 2003, Chelsea fans voted him their greatest ever player.

The "off-the-shoulder" striker

A forward who specializes in timing his runs so that he is only just onside when the ball is played forward to him is known as an "off-the-shoulder" striker. This is because he stays directly parallel with the opposing team's last defender, only moving off the shoulder at the last possible moment.

Patience required

As the off-the-shoulder striker is often ruled offside (correctly or otherwise), patience is a key requirement. Fans also need to be patient as the technique employed by these forwards can be frustrating to watch. However, when it works, the tactic can be highly effective, as it offers the striker a crucial head start over defenders. AC Milan's Pippo Inzaghi is one of the greatest off-the-shoulder strikers.

> 66 THE OFF-THE-SHOULDER STRIKER **IS JUST ONSIDE WHEN THE BALL** IS PLAYED **FORWARD** TO HIM. 99

The striker hangs "off-the-shoulder" of the opponent's deepest-lying defender (shown in blue)

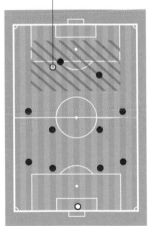

OFF-THE-SHOULDER STRIKER'S DOMAIN

The off-the-shoulder striker positions himself alongside the opposing team's last man (the last defender before the goalkeeper). From this position he is well placed to break through on goal.

THIERRY HENRY

At Arsenal, Thierry Henry evolved into a mixture of forward and winger. His approach is to drift to the left before cutting in and shooting. He often plays "off-the-shoulder."

The "poacher"

The poacher is a penalty-box opportunist who either quickly finds space to shoot, or picks up loose balls and toe-pokes them into the goal. While he may not always look like a conventional player, he is one of the most effective types of striker. He has a great goal-scoring ability and possesses excellent "off-the-ball" movements. He is renowned for his accurate close-range finishes.

Quick reactions

The poacher must possess extremely quick reactions. He needs to hone the knack of being in the right place at the right time and should be able to snatch goals close to the opposing team's penalty area.

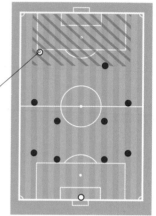

The poacher occupies the opposing team's penalty area, where he aims to score opportunistic goals

THE POACHER'S DOMAIN

The poacher is an extremely forward-lying striker, focusing his attentions on the opponent's penalty area. He looks to exploit any goal-scoring opportunities that present themselves.

> ❝ THE POACHER IS A **PENALTY-BOX OPPORTUNIST** WHO EITHER QUICKLY FINDS SPACE TO SHOOT, **OR PICKS UP LOOSE BALLS** AND TOE-POKES THEM INTO THE GOAL. ❞

Striking partnerships

Strikers often work in pairs to form effective partnerships. The best duos consist of players with differing styles, much like the partnerships between central defenders (see p.45). One well-tested formula places a tall, powerful player with a smaller, more agile one. The larger player wins headers and sets up goals for his partner, or tries to retain the ball to bring him more into play.

Great pairings

The greatest striking partnerships are based on more than just complementary playing styles—the players must instinctively know what the other will do in any given situation. This can be achieved by experience, but there is another more elusive ingredient—they must "click."

TELEPATHY EXPERIMENT

In the 1970s, Liverpool forwards Kevin Keegan and John Toshack developed such an intrinsic partnership that they seemed telepathic. To test this, a TV station invited them into the studio to guess the shape drawn on a card by the other player. They guessed correctly every time. Later, Toshack confessed that they could see the shapes reflected in the cameras.

Unclassifiable strikers

Not all strikers can be neatly pigeonholed and this can be a positive advantage to a team. While the defending team can use a tall defender to mark a conventional target man, it will struggle to defend against a forward who defies categorization. For this reason, some of the greatest strikers have been mavericks with playing styles all of their own.

Versatility required

A striker who can vary his role during a game is rare but invaluable. Dutch star Robin Van Persie is a prime example. He is tall, quick, and capable of shooting from any angle and distance—attributes that allow him to play effectively on the left wing, in the "hole," or as a target man. By moving between these positions he can shake off his markers and create scoring opportunities for himself.

The unclassifiable striker frequently "cuts in" from the wing before shooting

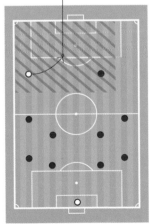

UNCLASSIFIABLE STRIKER'S DOMAIN

While it is difficult to place the unclassifiable striker, he often receives the ball on the wing before "cutting in" toward the center of the field and unleashing a shot.

ROBIN VAN PERSIE

Netherlands and Arsenal forward Robin van Persie is a creative and an "unclassifiable" striker.

Individual Skills

Anatomy of a player

Like dancers and singers, soccer players' bodies are their instruments, their means of performance and expression. Although professionals are generally getting taller and increasingly fitter, the game still offers space for a variety of physiques and specialisms.

Key requirements

Although players vary in size and shape, all top-level players have certain anatomical requirements in common. Strong leg muscles—the calf, thigh muscles, and hamstrings—are the most important. Good upper-body strength is also vital.

Eyes
Players need to read the game and judge speeds and distances

Deltoids
These muscles power the arms and are useful for cushioning high balls

Chest muscles
This muscle group helps players to run and pass

Abdominals
Core inner-body strength is a prerequisite of the balance and posture required for top-level soccer

Quadriceps
The four muscles at the front of the thigh are the soccer player's engine room, essential for running and kicking

Ankles
Must be strong to cope with the stress of constant changes of direction

Groin
Takes much of the muscle stress caused by shooting, so pre-match stretching is vital

" A PLAYER'S **NECK MUSCLES** ARE THE KEY TO POWERFUL HEADING. "

BODY STRENGTH
A player's leg muscles do much of the work (and are the most prone to injury), but a strong neck, spine, chest, abdominals, and deltoids are all important.

Neck muscles
The key to powerful heading, players need to work specifically on these muscles to strengthen them

Spine
Liable to take a lot of stress in a match, as a player braces and stretches for every turn

Hamstrings
Give flexibility to the knee and hip and allow the leg to stretch. These are easily torn, so players need them to be long, supple, and tough

Calves
Raise the heel when running, walking, and jumping. The calf muscles are very prone to cramps

Achilles heel
Has to take all the strain of soccer's bursts of speed, stop and start motion, and sharp turns

Changing shape

Soccer players are changing shape. One study looked at the height, weight, and body mass index (BMI) of players in the top English division between 1974 and 2004. Over those 30 years, players on average have become taller and leaner.

Highs and lows

Soccer does not favor one body type or one kind of player. Since it demands a complex range and mixture of skills, it can accommodate all shapes and sizes. Many different physical makeups have played at the top level, from towering strikers to tiny midfield terriers.

> " DIEGO MARADONA'S **LOW CENTER OF GRAVITY** GAVE HIM **AMAZING BALANCE**. "

THE LONG...	...AND THE SHORT
6ft 10in (2.08m) Kristof van Hout (Belgium)	5ft 3in (1.60m) Brian Flynn (Wales)
6ft 9in (2.05m) Yang Changpeng (China)	5ft 2in (1.58m) Élton Jose Xavier Gomes (Brazil)
6ft 8in (2.04m) Tor Hogne Aarøy (Norway)	5ft 1in (1.55m) Jafal Rashed (Qatar)

6ft 7in
2.01m

5ft 5in
1.65m

PETER CROUCH
Tall, gangly, but surprisingly mobile and a regular for England.

DIEGO MARADONA
His low center of gravity gave him amazing balance.

The perfect player?

Despite 150 years of top-flight soccer, the perfect player
has yet to grace the field. Hypothetically, however, it would
be rewarding to create the perfect identikit player by fusing
together the best physical attributes of some of the game's greats.

PART	WHO AND WHY?
BRAIN	Johan Cruyff—dubbed "Pythagoras in Boots"; no player ever saw the angles and spaces of a game more quickly.
HANDS	Pat Jennings—huge, long-fingered, and reliable, the Northern Ireland keeper even scored a goal in 1967.
UPPER BODY	Christian Vieri—the powerful chest of the Italian striker gives him the strength to out-jump and out-muscle defenders.
THIGHS	Ronald Koeman—very muscular upper legs, so the Dutch player delivered shots and free-kicks with great force.
RIGHT FOOT	David Beckham—a foot that can caress and coax the ball as well as slam it is the perfect tool.
LEFT FOOT	Maradona—the Argentinian scored the "Goal of the Century" with his left foot, and produced many other magical moments.

6ft 4in
1.93m

5ft 8in
1.73m

FATTY FOULKES
At his peak in the
1920s, Foulkes weighed
280lbs (127kg).

PELÉ
The perfect player,
a balance of height,
speed, and power.

Warming up

Every game of soccer should start with a warm-up. Soccer's twists and turns and its demand for fast accelerating movements will quickly pull or damage cold muscles, and stiff joints and tendons. Similarly, the body's metabolism works best if it is gradually coaxed into life, by systematically raising the heart rate and body temperature of the player. There are four stages to the typical warm-up routine used by professional teams—jogging and gentle stretches, static stretches, dynamic stretches, and footwork and agility. The session is always followed by a cool-down.

Stage 1: jogging and gentle stretches

To get the body ready for the demanding tasks ahead, start by raising your body temperature, pushing up your heart rate, and beginning the process of stretching tendons and mobilizing joints.

Teamwork
Working in pairs, jog around a 30ft (10m) circle, slowing at intervals to stretch

Side step
Take two steps to one side, then back again; begin to work the leg muscle, back, and torso

Stage 2: static stretches

The body is warm, but big muscle groups are not yet ready for a full workout. The quadriceps in the front of the thigh and the hamstrings in the back of the leg need stretching. Groins, calves, and ankles may be damaged if used when cold.

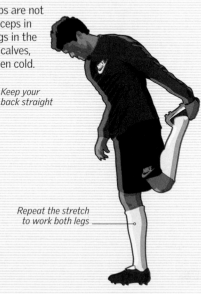

Keep your back straight

Repeat the stretch to work both legs

CALF STRETCH
Stand with your back foot flat on the floor and transfer weight to the front foot. Hold for about 10 seconds.

QUAD STRETCH
Hold your heel against your buttock for at least 30 seconds. Use a wall to aid balance.

Over the gate
Lift the knee and turn it inward. Swivel forward, switching sides with each lift

Kick out
Lift the knee high, then extend the lower leg as if kicking to stretch the hamstrings

30ft (10m)

Open the gate
Lift each knee to hip height and turn it outward to stretch the groin muscles. Swivel on the move forward

Hand/heel tap
Tap the hand on the heel, working the ankle joints and calf muscles

SPIRITUAL FOOTBALL

Yoga, the ancient Indian art of stretching, breathing, and meditation has been used by several famous players to help them recover from injury and to prolong their careers. Practitioners have included Manchester United winger Ryan Giggs and England goalkeeper David James.

Do not bend your knee beyond the ankle

Feel the muscles of your front leg tighten

HAMSTRING STRETCH
Extend one leg in front with the foot flexed. Bend your other knee and lean forward slightly.

GROIN STRETCH
Good for inner thigh and groin muscles—hold the position for 10–20 seconds.

Stage 3: dynamic stretches

Pick up the pace now and combine aerobic work (which raises the activity rate of the heart and lungs) with full muscle stretches. Work in pairs, moving through a series of routines that push your heart rates upward. Use your partner for balance during the moves. The intention is also to raise the body's temperature by approximately 2°F (1°C).

Kick and twist
Make a short kicking motion at an angle of about 45 degrees to alternate sides

Mock strikes
Swing each leg as if striking an imaginary soccer ball, moving the leg muscles all the way back and through

Lunge walk
Stride forward, then bend the knee of your front leg and drop the knee of your back leg so that it touches the ground

Hip swivels
Jog sideways, swinging your arms and hips in opposite directions

> **AFTER THE MUSCLES HAVE WARMED UP** AND THE **JOINTS HAVE RELAXED**, YOU CAN MOVE ONTO FASTER, **SHARPER MOVEMENTS** MORE CLOSELY RELATED TO SOCCER.

Stage 4: footwork and agility

Now that the muscles have warmed up and the joints have relaxed, you can move onto faster, sharper movements more closely related to actual game play. Work concentrates on the feet and ankles and higher-tempo movements.

Quick feet
Lift your legs quickly over the low hurdles with minimum bend

Side-to-side skip
Twist and turn at a high pace to keep your heart rate up

High knee touches
Keep stretching and working your hamstrings

Slalom
Jog backward through the pole slalom; this practices your balance and spatial awareness

Cone work
Move between the cone with sharp side steps; this works your ankle joints

Back steps
Jog slowly backward, moving from side to side, this works your hips and upper body

The cool-down

After training, you need to lower your heart rate and body temperature steadily, and allow your body to disperse the buildup of lactic acid that forms in well worked muscles. Repeat the gentle stretches at a steadily lower pace. Then repeat long static and dynamic stretching of all the key muscle groups.

COOL-DOWN ROUTINE		
STAGE ONE GENTLE MOVEMENTS	**STAGE TWO STATIC STRETCHES**	**STAGE THREE DYNAMIC STRETCHES**
OVER THE GATE	QUADS	MOCK STRIKES
OPEN THE GATE	HAMSTRINGS	KICK AND TWIST
HAND TAP	CALVES	HIP SWIVELS
KICK-OUT	GROIN	LUNGE WALK
SIDE STEP		

Training

Top teams spend a great deal of time practicing with the ball. Some of this is devoted to rehearsing set pieces (see pp.160–63), but a major part of the average training session is given to honing basic ball skills, so that they become instinctive.

Ballwork

A good training session encompasses a variety of skills, exercises all the key muscle groups, and encourages teamwork. The drills shown here represent some of the infinite choices available to coaches.

> **BALLWORK DRILLS** SHOULD BE PRACTICED **AFTER YOU HAVE WARMED UP AND STRETCHED** YOUR MUSCLES.

KAKÁ

Brazilian legend Kaká is renowned for his close control and ball skills, a talent honed on the training field through his career from a junior level. His ability is such that in 2009 British club Manchester City was reportedly willing to pay $157 million to secure his services.

Post warm-up

Ballwork drills should be practiced after you have warmed up. There should be one ball for every two or three players and these should remain in play throughout the session.

KEY

● Player	--- Ball motion
— Player motion	▲ Cone
○ Ball	

PLYOMETRICS

Plyometric training is designed to develop the explosive muscle power needed for sudden bursts of acceleration, such as a forward chasing a ball. A good example is players jumping over a series of hurdles set narrowly apart.

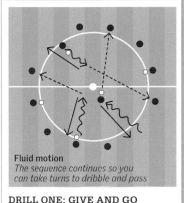

Fluid motion
The sequence continues so you can take turns to dribble and pass

DRILL ONE: GIVE AND GO

All players line up on the edge of a circle. Those with the ball dribble into the center, pass to players without the ball, and run back.

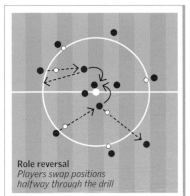

Role reversal
Players swap positions halfway through the drill

DRILL TWO: IN THE MIDDLE

Half the players stand on the outside of the circle, the other half toward its center. The two sets exchange passes with several balls.

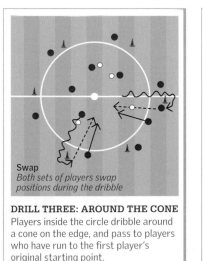

Swap
Both sets of players swap positions during the dribble

DRILL THREE: AROUND THE CONE

Players inside the circle dribble around a cone on the edge, and pass to players who have run to the first player's original starting point.

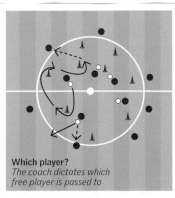

Which player?
The coach dictates which free player is passed to

DRILL FOUR: MORE CONE WORK

Players in the center dribble around cones. When instructed, they pass to a free player on the outside of the circle and swap positions.

Training without the ball

There are two aspects to training without the ball. The first consists of running and building stamina; players recovering from injuries also do strength work in the gym. The second concerns how players look after themselves away from the training field: diet, rest, and self-discipline are all important (see panel, opposite).

Building stamina

If a player runs out of energy toward the end of a match, the team is likely to suffer. Players need considerable stamina and their training should help them to develop it. A typical stamina-building session might consist of three 1,000yd (900m) runs followed by three of 660yd (600m) and three of 330yd (300m) with a two- to three-minute break between each run.

> **PLAYERS** REQUIRE **CONSIDERABLE STAMINA** THAT THEIR **TRAINING** HELPS THEM **DEVELOP**.

CARLOS QUIEROZ

Top coaches such as Carlos Quieroz help to motivate players during training sessions.

Sprint training

During matches, players sprint in quick bursts and spend the rest of the time jogging or walking. Sprint training is designed to reflect this. Players run flat-out for five to ten seconds, then walk back to the start and repeat the procedure. One of the advantages of this kind of training is that it accustoms the body to working anaerobically. This means that it is temporarily producing energy without oxygen, which is what happens when a player suddenly has to run flat-out at the end of 90 exhausting minutes. Anaerobic exercise is hard on the body so it should only be practiced occasionally, perhaps once every two weeks.

> ❝ SPRINT TRAINING **ACCUSTOMS THE BODY** TO TEMPORARILY PRODUCE **ENERGY WITHOUT OXYGEN**. ❞

FOODS TO EAT, DRINK, AND AVOID

If the wrong kind of fuel is put into a car it will underperform. The same is true of soccer players with regard to their diets. Players should eat and drink certain types of food to perform at their best on match days.

EAT

Players should consume plenty of carbohydrates (such as potatoes and pasta), as these provide the body with energy; easily digestible proteins such as fish and chicken; and vegetables rich in iron, such as broccoli.

● **After training**: The body stores energy in the form of a substance called glycogen. Players need to replenish their glycogen levels within two to five hours of exercising. The best way to do this is to eat plenty of carbohydrates.

● **Three days before a match**: Players should start "carbohydrate-loading." This means they should eat meals that comprise 75 percent complex carbohydrates.

● **Match day**: To help optimize energy available to the player during the game, he or she should eat a meal high in carbohydrates and low in protein and fat three to four hours before kick-off.

DRINK

Soccer players should drink lots of water, particularly before and after training sessions. Players can lose four quarts (four liters) or more of water during a match and will need to rehydrate themselves as quickly as possible. In addition to water, isotonic drinks containing vital nutrients and sugars are particularly easy for the body to absorb. There are several commercial varieties, but a simple version can be made with fruit juice and water mixed in equal measures.

AVOID

Players should avoid all caffeine (tea and coffee), alcohol, and junk foods (such as potato chips and deep-fried foodstuffs). Consumption of dairy products, and fatty and high-sugar foods should also be limited.

Controlling the ball

Possession is the key to controlling a game and a team can only be said to be in possession when one of its players has the ball under his control. Achieving this is one of the fundamental skills of soccer. No matter how perfectly a pass is delivered, it will be wasted if you fail to control the ball effectively.

Flexibility and first touch

Controlling the ball is easiest when it is passed gently to the feet but you must be prepared to reach it at any height, from any angle, and at any speed. The quality of a player's first touch is crucial. The best players are able to put the ball exactly where they want it with the same touch they use to bring it under control, giving them time and space to consider their next move.

Using the body

If you receive the ball at a level too high to control with your feet, you have three main options: to use your thigh, chest, or head. An excellent way to practice these skills is via a game of "head tennis." Played over a volleyball net, you must keep the ball from touching the ground, and return it over the net by using your head, chest, thigh, and feet. The more frequently you play this enjoyable game, the better your skills will become.

Your thigh should be about 45 degrees to the ground when the ball arrives

CONTROL WITH THIGH
If you can "catch" the ball with the upper part of your thigh, you can bring it under control very effectively.

SHANKLY'S SWEAT BOX

Liverpool's legendary manager Bill Shankly used an innovative but exhausting device to improve his players' ball control and stamina. Known as the "sweat box," it consisted of an area bounded by four numbered boards, which players shot against, in between controlling the rebounds, corresponding to the number shouted out by the trainer.

SYLVAIN WILTORD

The French international demonstrates the athleticism involved in certain ball control maneuvers. Wiltord has effectively caught the ball at shoulder height with the toe of his cleat. Players must have both excellent coordination and suppleness to accomplish this.

> THE QUALITY OF A PLAYER'S **FIRST TOUCH IS CRUCIAL**. THE BEST PLAYERS ARE ABLE TO **PUT THE BALL EXACTLY WHERE THEY WANT IT**.

Lean back to take away the ball's momentum

Relax your neck muscles to cushion the ball

Jump up to anticipate the ball

CONTROL WITH CHEST

Using the chest to control the ball is easier than it sounds. You must take care to keep the ball from hitting you too low and winding you.

CONTROL WITH HEAD

This technique is difficult because the skull is hard, making a degree of bounce inevitable, but sometimes you will have no alternative.

Using the feet

The easiest way to control the ball with your feet is to get into a position to receive the ball early. To practice this, kick a ball against a wall at varying heights, strengths, and angles, and control the rebound. As you improve, ask a friend to rebound the ball for you so you have to make quick adjustments. Basic foot-trapping techniques involve the inside and sole of the foot (see below). Gradually, you will be able to move on to the outside, top, and side volley trap (see opposite).

Pull your foot back slightly to cushion impact

FOOT TENNIS

A good way to learn ball control is to use a tennis ball. Many great players honed their techniques in this way. If you can master a small, bouncy object such as a tennis ball, a regular soccer ball will seem as big as a pumpkin.

INSIDE OF FOOT

This is the easiest way to control the ball. Ideally, the ball will land about a stride ahead of you rather than directly at your feet.

As the ball lands, bring your foot down on it gently but firmly

IF YOU ARE ABLE TO MASTER A SMALL, BOUNCY TENNIS BALL, A REGULAR SOCCER BALL WILL SEEM AS BIG AS A PUMPKIN.

SOLE OF FOOT

A ball dropping near your feet is best controlled by pinning it to the ground with the underside of the foot.

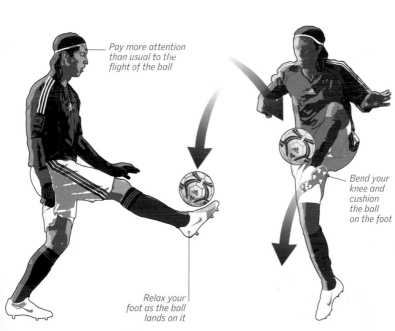

> **YOU CAN PRACTICE CONTROLLING THE BALL** WITH YOUR FEET BY **KICKING A BALL AGAINST A WALL** AT VARYING **HEIGHTS, STRENGTHS,** AND **ANGLES**.

Relaxing the leg too much at the moment of impact could result in a jarred knee

OUTSIDE OF FOOT
If the close proximity of opponents precludes using the inside of the favored foot, use the outside of the other foot.

Pay more attention than usual to the flight of the ball

Bend your knee and cushion the ball on the foot

Relax your foot as the ball lands on it

TOP-OF-FOOT CUSHION
A way to control a dropping ball, this is a difficult tactic to perform correctly, since you have to use the narrowest part of your foot.

SIDE VOLLEY TRAP
This is used when the ball arrives too high to trap but too low to chest down. The technique requires flexibility for good execution.

Passing

Passing is the lifeblood of any team and a vital skill for all players to learn, including goalkeepers. There are several good reasons why you might choose to pass—to clear the ball from a danger area, to help your team keep possession, or to try to set up a scoring opportunity, for example. There is only one good time for you to make the pass, however, whenever there is a teammate in a better position than you.

Types of pass

Players pass in order to develop attacks, or to work the ball away from opponents. These passes can be along the ground or in the air, over short distances or long range. Short passes are the easiest to execute; long-range airborne passes the most difficult. Each type of pass has its advantages and disadvantages.

PASSING OPTIONS
Short passes are sometimes made in tight situations when the player in possession is near the opponent's goal, or laterally between defenders prior to searching a forward pass. Inswinging, outswinging, and driven passes are made over long distances. They are usually executed from the player's own half of the field.

KEY
- - Inswinging pass
- - Outswinging pass
- - Driven pass
- - Short pass
- - Channel pass
● Player

USING THE CHANNELS

Sometimes, when you have ball possession, there may be no obvious teammate to pass the ball to. In such cases, you should either run with the ball or pass it into a "safe" channel (usually directly ahead of you, see above) which gives a teammate a realistic chance of winning the race with the defender to receive it.

Short pass

This pass is the most accurate kind for two reasons: the ball is struck with the side of the foot; and any slight miscue can be masked by the small distance the ball has to travel.

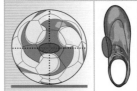

WHERE TO STRIKE THE BALL

Place your standing leg alongside the ball with your toes pointing in the direction of travel

1 Approach the ball at a 30-degree angle, giving yourself room to swing your passing leg.

Strike the ball with the side of your foot for maximum control

2 Strike the ball with the side of your foot and keep the ball down. Keep your ankle firm.

Watch the ball closely as it heads to its target

3 The length of follow-through reflects the weight you want to give the pass.

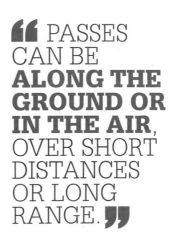

❝ PASSES CAN BE ALONG THE GROUND OR IN THE AIR, OVER SHORT DISTANCES OR LONG RANGE. ❞

Making a long pass

Long passes or crosses can be very effective, largely because defenders tend to guard their opponents less thoroughly the farther away they are from the action. Accuracy in executing this pass is crucial as any error will be magnified.

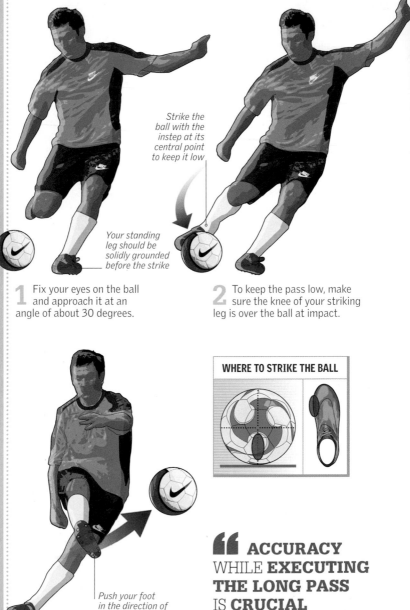

Strike the ball with the instep at its central point to keep it low

Your standing leg should be solidly grounded before the strike

1 Fix your eyes on the ball and approach it at an angle of about 30 degrees.

2 To keep the pass low, make sure the knee of your striking leg is over the ball at impact.

WHERE TO STRIKE THE BALL

Push your foot in the direction of the ball after impact

3 Your follow-through should be more pronounced than for a short pass.

❝ ACCURACY WHILE **EXECUTING THE LONG PASS** IS **CRUCIAL** AS ANY **ERROR** WILL BE **MAGNIFIED**. **❞**

The science of spin

Spinning a ball is a skill every good player should know. Once struck, the ball naturally seeks the path of least resistance, swerving in the direction of the spin—to the right if the ball is spinning clockwise and left if it is spinning counterclockwise.

SIDEWAYS SPIN

If a ball is spinning through the air sideways, one side of it will move in the direction of its flight while the other will move counter to it. The forward-spinning side develops a greater force than the backward-spinning one. This is called the Magnus force.

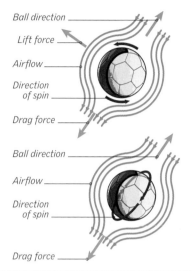

Ball direction
Lift force
Airflow
Direction of spin
Drag force

TOP- AND BACKSPIN

If a ball is rotating forward or backward, the same principle applies but it has different effects. A ball given topspin will move downward faster than it otherwise would, while the reverse is true of a ball given backspin.

Ball direction
Airflow
Direction of spin
Drag force

Adding curve to a long pass

Putting curve onto the ball can be useful during attacking moves because the path of a curving ball is much harder to anticipate, and therefore defend, than one that flies straight.

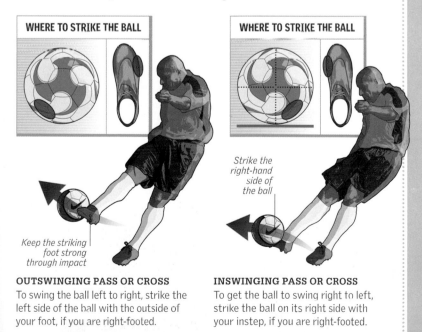

WHERE TO STRIKE THE BALL

WHERE TO STRIKE THE BALL

Strike the right-hand side of the ball

Keep the striking foot strong through impact

OUTSWINGING PASS OR CROSS

To swing the ball left to right, strike the left side of the ball with the outside of your foot, if you are right-footed.

INSWINGING PASS OR CROSS

To get the ball to swing right to left, strike the ball on its right side with your instep, if you are right-footed.

Running with the ball

Running with the ball under control is known as dribbling. In its basic form, the skill involves you kicking the ball ahead of yourself, running to catch up with it, kicking it forward again and so on. In practice, however, you will rarely have clear spaces ahead of you for long as opposing defenders will arrive to try to check your runs. You, therefore, need to keep the ball close to your feet and develop a repertoire of skills to avoid would-be tacklers.

Beating opponents

As a dribbler, you may employ a variety of techniques to get past opponents without checking your runs. One of the most important is the shoulder drop, in which you lower the level of one shoulder to fool the defender into thinking you are heading in that direction. Another is having the ability to anticipate tackles (see pp.126-29) and the dexterity to jump over them.

Stop-turns while running

While dribbling, you will often want to change direction, either to develop a different angle of attack, run into space, or evade a defender. To do this, some of the most popular techniques are the inside and outside hooks, and the Puskás turn or drag back (see pp.82–83).

SIR STANLEY MATTHEWS

Sir Stanley Matthews (1915–2000), one of the greatest wingers in history, was famous for his body swerve.

How to dribble

The best dribblers give the impression that the ball is tied to their shoes. These players also have the ability to easily alternate between both feet (using the inside and outside of the feet). A dribble is executed as follows.

THE NUTMEG

The nutmeg is a maneuver in which an attacking player passes the ball through an opponent's legs, weighting it so he can continue his dribble on the other side. Defenders dislike being nutmegged, but if they keep their legs too close together to prevent it, they invite the attacker to kick the ball past them and get around them to the side.

> **KEEP THE BALL CLOSE TO YOUR FEET** AND **DEVELOP A REPERTOIRE OF SKILLS** TO AVOID WOULD-BE TACKLERS.

Don't kick the ball too hard with either foot

1 Using your left foot, gently kick the ball between 12 and 19in (30–50cm) ahead of you and to the right.

Keep the ball close by

2 Keep your eyes on the ball while running forward, occasionally looking up to assess the situation ahead of you.

Keep your eyes alternately on the ball and the space ahead

Push the ball forward with your right foot

3 When you reach the ball, continue with the dribble, using your right foot. Repeat this sequence, using your left foot then right.

Inside hook

This hook technique is easier than the outside hook (see below). It is used to move inside (to the left for a right-footer) when an opponent is on your outside.

1 Start the inside hook by dribbling forward with the ball under close control, while paying attention to the presence of defenders.

Keep light on your feet at this stage of the dribble

Outside hook

This skill is more demanding than the inside hook (see above), since you must use the outside of your right foot to move 180 degrees to the right (for a right-footer).

1 As with the inside hook turn, start the maneuver by dribbling forward, feeding the ball between each foot alternately.

Puskás turn

Named after the great Hungarian striker Ferenc Puskás, this trick involves a quarter turn that allows you have to rapidly move at right angles to the direction in which you were originally dribbling.

1 Start with the ball in line with the center of your body, then swing one foot forward as if to kick the ball.

Make as if to kick the ball forward

2 Place one foot slightly ahead of the ball and use the instep to push the ball in the direction you wish to turn.

Twist your foot around the outside of the ball

3 Spin to the left, push off your back foot, using your front foot to continue the dribble away from your opponent.

Ensure your standing foot is planted solidly for the spin

Use your arms to keep steady

Use the outside of your foot

2 Using the outside of your foot, hook the ball back in the direction you wish to go.

3 Turn 180 degrees to the right then push off with your back foot and accelerate away, using the front foot to continue the dribble.

Use your arms to power the run

Kick the ball to the front

2 However, rather than kicking the ball forward, move your foot slightly over the ball and bring the cleats into contact with its top.

Abbreviate the kick and rest the cleats on the ball

3 Putting your weight on the other foot, drag the ball back and then knock it sideways with the outside of your shoe.

Pull the ball back with the studs, then move into space

Stepovers

The stepover, also known as the scissors maneuver, is one of the most visually striking moves in soccer. It is used to fool an opponent into thinking that you are about to pass sideways when you are in possession, whereas, in fact, you just continue your run. Stepovers were considered an exotic skill, but in recent years they have become almost commonplace.

Types of stepover

In the classic stepover, you move while in possession as if to push the ball one way with the outside of one foot, but actually pass the foot over and around the ball (from inside to outside) without touching it before picking it up with the other foot and moving in the opposite direction. There are two more developed styles of the stepover—the Rivelino (see opposite) and the double stepover (see pp.86–87).

CRISTIANO RONALDO

Portuguese winger Cristiano Ronaldo, criticized for excessive showmanship early in his career, is currently the undisputed master of the stepover. In 2008, he netted 42 goals in all competitions, winning the UEFA Golden Shoe Award for the top scorer in a European league.

The Rivelino

In this variation of the stepover, named after the Brazilian winger, the legs move around the ball in the opposite direction, that is from outside to inside. The Rivelino requires precise balance.

Keep your eyes focused on the ball to avoid contact with either foot

Move your left hip forward

Pul your left foot down

Dribble slowly

1 Dribble the ball slowly toward the defender. Plant your front foot and bring the trailing leg toward the ball.

2 Instead of making contact with the ball, bring the trailing leg up and over the ball, placing it on the other side.

Raise your right shoulder and move to the left

Place your weight on your right side before springing off

3 Swivel 180 degrees, place your weight on the right foot, then play the ball with your left.

" STEPOVERS ARE USED TO FOOL AN OPPONENT INTO THINKING THAT YOU WILL PASS SIDEWAYS WHEN YOU ACTUALLY CONTINUE YOUR RUN. "

Double stepover

In the double stepover, you have to perform the trick twice in quick succession, once with each foot. Technically, this is a more difficult tactic to master.

> **IN SOUTH AMERICA**, THE CONTINENT WHICH **GAVE BIRTH TO THE STEPOVER**, IT IS CALLED THE **PEDALADA**, AND WAS A COMMON SKILL USED BY **BRAZILIAN LEGEND PELÉ**.

Keep your eyes on the ball

Dribble forward at a slow pace

1 Dribble the ball forward and prepare to set your standing leg.

Keep your eyes on the ball

Lift your left foot in a circle over the ball

Ball keeps moving forward

4 Perform a second stepover, this time with the left foot and in a counterclockwise direction.

5 You will again be back to the starting position, but farther forward than before.

Drop your left shoulder

Lift and rotate your right foot through 360 degrees

2 Then move your right foot around and over the ball in a clockwise direction.

3 This will bring you back to the starting point, but farther forward than before.

Spring off from the left side to travel quickly to the right

6 Knock the ball forward with your right foot and continue the dribble.

MASTER OF THE STEPOVER
Cristiano Ronaldo performed 11 stepovers per game on average during the 2007–08 season.

SPACE CREATED
The typical amount of space created by an effective stepover move is 25in (63cm).

GREAT EVASION
Brazil winger Denílson made six stepovers before evading France midfielder Emmanuel Petit during the 1998 World Cup.

INVENTOR OF THE MOVE
Pelé, the inventor of the stepover, has won the World Cup three times.

STEP IT UP
In 2007 Roma's Mancini performed six stepovers in rapid succession to score a goal against Olympique Lyonnais.

Spins and turns

Some of the most spectacular moves in soccer involve players spinning or turning in unexpected ways. These require great technical accuracy and often only the world's best known and most skillful players use them successfully in a match situation.

Finding space

Complex turns are more challenging than the turns covered under the dribbling section (see pp.80–83) and need lots of practice. Making a successful turn is a great way to lose a marker or wrong-foot an opponent, both of which will buy you time to run into space or make a considered pass to a teammate. Two of the best maneuvers for achieving this are the Zidane spin and the Cruyff turn.

The Zidane spin

The Zidane spin is a form of pirouette in which you have to spin through 360 degrees while keeping the ball under close control. It is as difficult to describe as it is to do, but can be broken down into five stages. Zidane has performed this technique at the highest level on many occasions. If executed well, it can buy you good time in crowded midfield situations.

Start the spin with your favored foot

1 Dribble forward with the ball as normal, then stop and put your stronger foot on top of it.

Spin counter-clockwise

Place your weaker foot on the ball after spinning

2 Roll the ball backward, spin 180 degrees around it, then collect it with your weaker foot.

Complete the spin

Swap feet again after spinning

3 Roll the ball back gently with your weaker foot and turn 180 degrees in the same direction.

4 After completing the full spin, collect the ball again with your stronger foot.

Protect the ball from defenders

5 Finally, continue with your run, leaving the opposition defenders perplexed.

Continue dribbling in the same direction in which you started the spin

Use outstretched arms for balance during the spin and to repel the advances of opponents

> ❝ THE ZIDANE SPIN IS A **FORM OF PIROUETTE** IN WHICH YOU HAVE TO **SPIN THROUGH 360 DEGREES** WHILE KEEPING THE BALL UNDER CLOSE CONTROL. ❞

ZINÉDINE ZIDANE

Zinédine Zidane gained worldwide prominence at Juventus in Italy and then Real Madrid in Spain. His achievements include being a World Cup winner in 1998, and a three-time FIFA World Player of the Year.

The Cruyff turn

This maneuver, a complex drag back that always leaves defenders behind, is named after Netherlands forward Johan Cruyff. When executing this tactic, your goal is to feign execution of a long pass or cross but instead spin 180 degrees and continue the dribble.

" JOHAN CRUYFF, KNOWN AS PYTHAGORAS IN BOOTS, FIRST PERFORMED THE CRUYFF TURN IN 1974. "

JOHAN CRUYFF

Cruyff was the most complete player in the Dutch and Ajax teams famous for "total soccer." Nominally a striker, he bamboozled markers by dropping into midfield. His vision and passing skills led to the accolade "Pythagoras in boots." This Dutch maestro perfected a move known as the "Cruyff turn," which he first performed in 1974.

THE HALF-PREKI

Predrag Radosavljevi began his career with Red Star Belgrade and ended it in Major League Soccer in the US, where he shortened his name to Preki. In this maneuver, named after him, you can create space, while dribbling, between you and an approaching defender by rolling the ball across the front of your body with the sole of your dominant foot. When you lift your foot to begin the move, the defender might think you will pass. Another version of the trick starts with a half-Preki and ends with a stepover (see pp.84–87).

Pass your foot over the ball rather than striking it

Plant your standing foot solidly, since this forms a strong base for the move

Push the ball gently behind you with your right foot

1 Plant one foot by the ball and make as if to shoot or hit a long pass with your other leg.

2 Bring the leg toward the ball, but instead of kicking it, pass your foot over the ball.

Turn your body 90 degrees

Plant the weight on your right side and use this as a springboard

3 Using the inside of the same foot, drag the ball back behind you and turn your body.

4 Complete the turn through 180 degrees and run off with the ball.

❝ PLANT ONE FOOT BY THE BALL, AS IF TO HIT A LONG PASS WITH THE OTHER LEG. ❞

Fakes

Deception is a vital ingredient in top-class soccer. Many of the most effective moves rely on players fooling their opponents into thinking they are going to do one thing and actually doing another. When this works, it cons members of the other team into moving out of position and buys crucial time for the team in possession.

Types of fake

"Selling" someone a dummy—acting as if to kick the ball but in fact leaving it to run on, usually to a teammate—is one of the most common forms of fakes in soccer. But there are also several others, including shuffles, fake kicks, and "flip-flaps." All have the effect of confusing and wrong-footing the opponent.

RONALDINHO

Few players have had as many tricks at their disposal as Brazilian striker Ronaldinho. He is a master of deception, using his eyes and a range of tricks, flicks, and dummies. He is one of the few players who uses freestyle techniques in top-flight matches.

The fake kick

In this fake, you have to mime a shot or a pass, causing the defenders to flinch, but instead you simply pass your foot over or just to the side of the ball. This gives you time and space to turn or deliver a pass.

Wind up your foot for a strong kick

1 Give every indication of taking a long-range shot at goal or making a long pass. Draw back your leg in preparation for a strike.

Keep your eyes on the ball

Practice slowing down your foot before the ball

2 Swing your foot down hard, but as it approaches the ball, slow it down rapidly and pass the foot over the ball.

Drag the ball away from the opponent

3 While your opponent turns away in anticipation of a shot, place your foot lightly on top of the ball and drag it back quickly.

FOR A FAKE KICK, **MIME A SHOT OR A PASS**, BUT ACTUALLY **PASS YOUR FOOT OVER** OR **JUST TO THE SIDE** OF THE BALL.

The elastico
or flip-flap

Brazil striker Ronaldinho is associated particularly with the "elastico" or "flip-flap." It involves you moving your foot very quickly from right to left while dribbling, keeping the ball in such close proximity that it appears connected to your foot by elastic.

WHY BRAZIL?

Brazilian players are famous for their eye-catching tricks on the field. Why they are so famous is down to their unique soccer philosophy. In addition to being tactically astute, Brazilian players like to produce the unexpected, doing simple things with flair, and playing for the sheer fun and joy of the game.

Make the defender think you're heading to the right

Ball should be rolling forwards

1 Prepare for the elastico by looking in the direction you want the approaching defender to think you are about to play the ball.

The Beardsley shuffle

The most famous shuffle in sport, a high-speed shimmy that mesmerized opponents, belonged to Muhammad Ali. The soccer equivalent, essentially an abbreviated stepover (see pp.84–87), was perfected by Peter Beardsley.

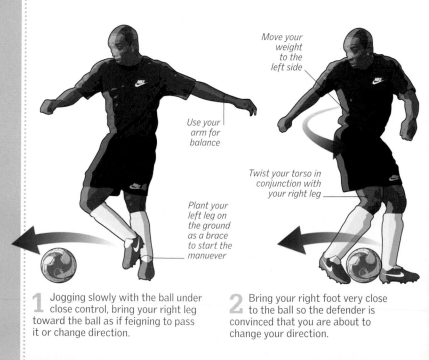

Use your arm for balance

Plant your left leg on the ground as a brace to start the maneuver

Move your weight to the left side

Twist your torso in conjunction with your right leg

1 Jogging slowly with the ball under close control, bring your right leg toward the ball as if feigning to pass it or change direction.

2 Bring your right foot very close to the ball so the defender is convinced that you are about to change your direction.

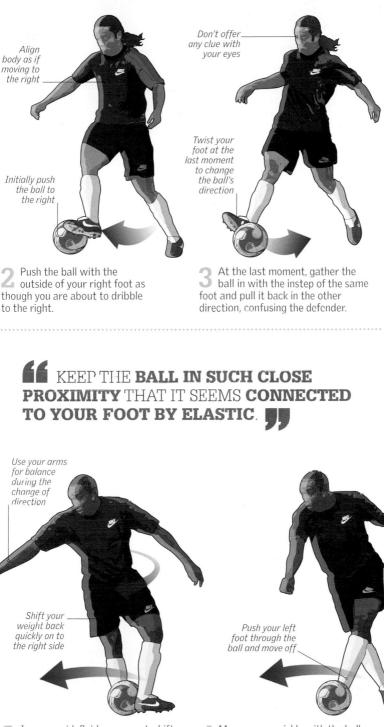

Align body as if moving to the right

Don't offer any clue with your eyes

Twist your foot at the last moment to change the ball's direction

Initially push the ball to the right

2 Push the ball with the outside of your right foot as though you are about to dribble to the right.

3 At the last moment, gather the ball in with the instep of the same foot and pull it back in the other direction, confusing the defender.

> KEEP THE **BALL IN SUCH CLOSE PROXIMITY** THAT IT SEEMS **CONNECTED TO YOUR FOOT BY ELASTIC**.

Use your arms for balance during the change of direction

Shift your weight back quickly on to the right side

Push your left foot through the ball and move off

3 In one rapid, fluid movement, shift your balance back to the right side, leaving the defender confused as to your chosen path.

4 Move away quickly with the ball in the direction you were traveling in in step 1. You will gain precious space as a result.

Shooting

Soccer would be nothing without goals. Besides heading the ball, benefiting from an own goal, or a lucky deflection, the only way to score is to shoot. This can be done from almost any position on the field, but the closer you are to the opponents' goal when you take a shot the higher the chances of success. There are many ways of scoring a goal; however, always strike the ball as hard as you can without sacrificing accuracy.

The basic shot

Certain principles apply whether a shot is long- or short-range, placed, or blasted. You should aim the ball either side of the goalkeeper and keep it down, so it doesn't fly over the crossbar.

Sweep your striking leg through on a plane consistent with the ball's direction

Open your leg and strike the ball on the instep

WHERE TO STRIKE THE BALL

1 Place your standing foot firmly next to the ball and pointing toward the goal.

2 Make contact with the center of the ball or a spot slightly below it.

The curving shot

A difficult shot to execute well, it requires a highly precise strike, both in terms of the part of the foot used and the impact position on the ball. For the inswinging strike (see right), connect with the instep on the base of the ball; for the outswinger, use the same spot on the outside of your foot (see also p.79).

WHERE TO STRIKE THE BALL

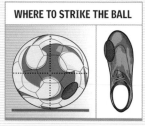

Use your standing foot as a solid base from which to swing your striking leg

1 Approach the ball and ensure that your standing leg is about 18in (45cm) to the side.

The chip, scoop, and lob

When a goalkeeper is off his line, there is a chance of beating him by lofting the ball over his head and weighting the shot so that the ball drops under the crossbar. The three methods by which you can achieve this—the chip, scoop, and lob—are all about touch, timing, and judgment.

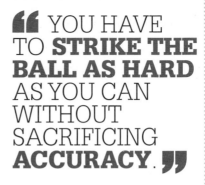

❝ YOU HAVE TO STRIKE THE BALL AS HARD AS YOU CAN WITHOUT SACRIFICING ACCURACY. ❞

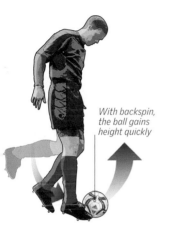

With backspin, the ball gains height quickly

THE CHIP AND SCOOP
You use the chip and the scoop when the ball is on the ground as the shot is taken. The chip requires back-lift and the scoop doesn't.

Strike the ball with finesse on top of your foot

THE LOB
Use the lob when the ball arrives at you full toss or after bouncing. You need to strike the ball with enough height to clear the goalkeeper.

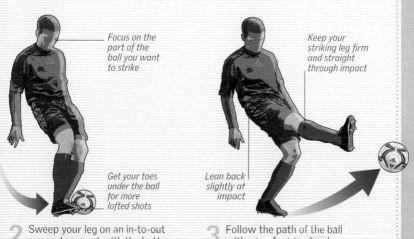

Focus on the part of the ball you want to strike

Get your toes under the ball for more lofted shots

2 Sweep your leg on an in-to-out arc and connect with the bottom right portion of the ball.

Keep your striking leg firm and straight through impact

Lean back slightly at impact

3 Follow the path of the ball with your foot to stand a better chance of curving it.

Volleying

There are few sights in soccer as satisfying as seeing a cleanly hit volley fly into the net. This technique, defined as striking a ball that is in full flight, is also used to make rapid crosses, clearances, and passes. A high level of foot-eye coordination is essential for volleying. When it is executed well, the results can be spectacular.

Volleying styles
The first type of volley is the full volley, where the ball is struck "on the fly." The second is the half-volley, where the ball is struck shortly after it has bounced. A third technique, the bicycle (or overhead) kick is normally performed by experienced, very athletic players.

The full volley

You use the full volley when the ball arrives at you without touching the ground. A well-executed full volley requires good timing, composure, and concentration.

Bend your knee in preparation for the strike

Plant your standing leg firmly on the ground to act as a pivot

1 Keep your eyes on the ball. Position yourself in its line of flight to stand the best chance of making good contact.

The half-volley

You perform the half-volley when the ball bounces just before you strike it. It is, therefore, sometimes on the rise at the moment of impact. If you can hit the ball at the exact moment it touches the ground the shot gains more momentum as the ball has lost less energy through not bouncing.

Prepare your body for the dropping ball as timing is everything

1 Watch the ball closely as it drops toward you. Position yourself and pull back your striking leg before connecting with the ball.

> **REPEATEDLY STRIKE A BALL SUSPENDED AT CHEST HEIGHT FROM A CROSSBAR VIA A PIECE OF ROPE TO PRACTICE THE FULL VOLLEY.**

2 Starting with your knee, bring your leg toward the ball and turn your hips. Strike the ball above center to keep it down.

3 Follow through with your kicking leg parallel to the ground and rotate your hips through the impact area.

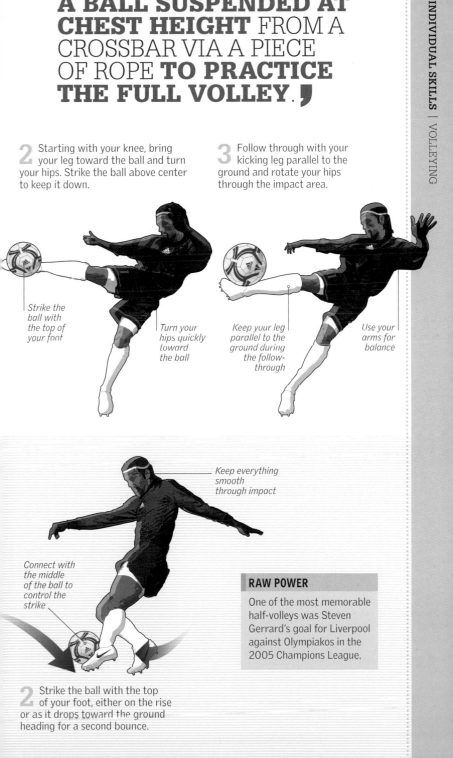

Strike the ball with the top of your foot

Turn your hips quickly toward the ball

Keep your leg parallel to the ground during the follow-through

Use your arms for balance

Keep everything smooth through impact

Connect with the middle of the ball to control the strike

RAW POWER

One of the most memorable half-volleys was Steven Gerrard's goal for Liverpool against Olympiakos in the 2005 Champions League.

2 Strike the ball with the top of your foot, either on the rise or as it drops toward the ground heading for a second bounce.

Bicycle kick

Also known as the overhead kick, the bicycle kick is one of soccer's most spectacular techniques. It was invented in the Peruvian port of Callao during a game between the locals and some European sailors in the early 1900s. Residents of the city are known as Chalacos and "Chalaca," the Latin American term for the trick, literally means "from Callao."

❝ FOR AN OVERHEAD KICK, 'TEE' YOURSELF UP WITH YOUR BACK TO THE GOAL, FLICKING THE BALL UP TO STRIKE. THROW YOUR HEAD BACK TO AID THE LIFT. ❞

Making an overhead kick

You can use the bicycle kick when an apparently misplaced cross arrives behind you. Alternatively, you can "tee" yourself up for an overhead kick with your back to the goal by flicking the ball up to strike.

Throw your head back to aid lift and your body will follow

Use your striking leg as a springboard

1 Launch yourself into the air by raising your non-kicking leg and pushing off the ground with the other foot.

DIDIER DROGBA

The Ivorian striker was five years old when he left Abidjan to live in France. He played in lower divisions, initially as defender, then as forward. Drogba's muscular frame makes him adept at finding space to perform overhead kicks.

Sweep your leg toward the ball with controlled pace

2 Once you are airborne, swing your kicking leg beyond the other leg and toward the ball.

Use your hand to soften the impact of the landing

3 Make contact with the ball with your back parallel to the ground. You should practice this in training before attempting it in a match.

Heading

Heading the ball is counterintuitive for any young players learning the game, because they think it will hurt. However, it is an essential skill to master because, on an average, the ball is in the air for 30 percent of the match time.

Types of header
There are many different types of header—basic, flick, tactical, defensive, and diving. You need to practice all of them so you know which one to use in a match situation.

Basic header

The basic header is used for passing and attempts on goal. It is made with the forehead as this provides the most power and accuracy, and doesn't hurt, unlike heading with the top of your head. To get power on a header, bend your knees and arch your back as you jump for the ball, turning yourself into the shape of a bow. Tilt your head back initially, then bring it forward rapidly using your neck muscles.

> **❝** LEARNING HOW TO **HEAD THE BALL IS ESSENTIAL,** SINCE THE BALL IS **IN THE AIR** FOR ABOUT **30 PERCENT** OF THE **MATCH TIME**. **❞**

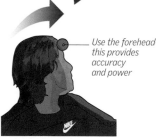

Keep your eyes on the ball

Use your arms to pull yourself into the air if you're jumping for the ball

Your head needs to swing downward at the moment of impact

Use the forehead— this provides accuracy and power

1 Get into position early and watch the ball come onto your head, keeping your eyes open throughout.

2 Without taking your eyes off the ball, tense your neck muscles to provide maximum power.

3 To head the ball downward at the moment of impact, you need to rise above the ball when you jump.

Flick header

The flick header is used to head the ball sideways or backward. It is useful when a defender facing upfield wants to head the ball back to his goalkeeper; when a midfielder wants to flick the ball back to a defender; or when a forward wants to get the ball into the penalty area from a near post cross or corner without revealing his intentions.

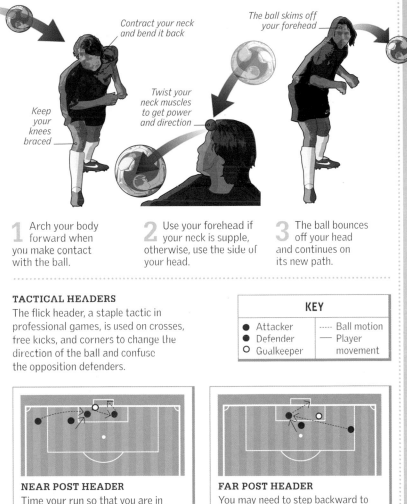

Contract your neck and bend it back

The ball skims off your forehead

Twist your neck muscles to get power and direction

Keep your knees braced

1 Arch your body forward when you make contact with the ball.

2 Use your forehead if your neck is supple, otherwise, use the side of your head.

3 The ball bounces off your head and continues on its new path.

TACTICAL HEADERS
The flick header, a staple tactic in professional games, is used on crosses, free kicks, and corners to change the direction of the ball and confuse the opposition defenders.

KEY	
● Attacker	----- Ball motion
● Defender	— Player
○ Goalkeeper	movement

NEAR POST HEADER
Time your run so that you are in front of your marker when the ball arrives, then flick it behind you into the area for a teammate.

FAR POST HEADER
You may need to step backward to lose your marker. You should direct your header back across goal toward the far post.

THE FLICK HEADER IS USED ON CROSSES, FREE KICKS, AND CORNERS TO CHANGE THE DIRECTION OF THE BALL.

Defensive header

The most important thing when making a defensive header is to get good height and distance on the ball. It is usually safer to direct it away from the center of the field.

WAYNE ROONEY

England's Wayne Rooney is one of the most skillful and powerful soccer players. He has extremely powerful neck muscles and knows how to put them to good use.

Time the jump so you connect with the ball before the attacker does

Head the ball as high and as far forwards as possible

Pass the ball to a teammate if possible

Connect at the top of your forehead to get height on the ball

Take care when landing

1 You should get in position early, since you will probably be competing with an attacker to get to the ball.

2 Make contact with the bottom half of the ball using the very top part of your forehead. Make sure you keep your neck braced.

3 If you approach the ball from a sideways position, you stand less chance of clashing with the attacker.

Diving header

Use your whole body as a battering ram to strike the ball. This skill is usually used only to attempt to score, since you face the risk of getting a kick in the face from a defender. It is an option when the ball arrives in front of you at a height between your neck and your knee.

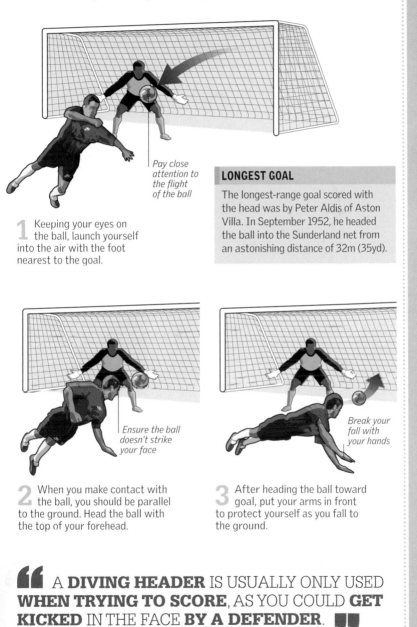

Pay close attention to the flight of the ball

1 Keeping your eyes on the ball, launch yourself into the air with the foot nearest to the goal.

LONGEST GOAL

The longest-range goal scored with the head was by Peter Aldis of Aston Villa. In September 1952, he headed the ball into the Sunderland net from an astonishing distance of 32m (35yd).

Ensure the ball doesn't strike your face

2 When you make contact with the ball, you should be parallel to the ground. Head the ball with the top of your forehead.

Break your fall with your hands

3 After heading the ball toward goal, put your arms in front to protect yourself as you fall to the ground.

❝ A **DIVING HEADER** IS USUALLY ONLY USED **WHEN TRYING TO SCORE**, AS YOU COULD **GET KICKED** IN THE FACE **BY A DEFENDER**. ❞

Throw-ins and corners

Statistically, corners and throw-ins are the most commonly awarded set pieces (see pp.160–63). A team is likely to make several of each during the course of a game. These can often lead to scoring opportunities—about a third of all goals are scored from set pieces—so coaches ensure players practice them extensively on the training ground.

Throw-ins

Throw-ins are used to restart play from the sideline. They can be taken either short or long. You need to be alert to the movements of your teammates and have a good aim when you throw. Throwing onto the field can be risky—if the opponents win possession they may quickly counterattack—so most throws are aimed upfield along the sideline, out of harm's way. The exception is the long throw aimed directly into the penalty area. This can be more potent than a corner as the thrown ball is delivered more accurately.

> **A MAJORITY OF THROWS ARE AIMED UPFIELD ALONG THE SIDELINE**, OUT OF HARM'S WAY. THE ONLY EXCEPTION IS THE LONG THROW.

RORY DELAP

Known as the "Delapidator," the Republic of Ireland player terrorizes defenses with his long throws. Delap throws the ball, on average, 125ft (38m).

Taking a throw-in

Throw-ins awarded in a team's own half are usually taken as a means of getting the ball back in play. But those taken near the opposition's penalty area can be as effective as a free-kick. There are three basic rules for taking throw-ins: you are permitted a run-up; you have to throw the ball from behind your head with both hands; and you must keep both your feet on the ground at the moment of release.

> " ABOUT **A THIRD OF ALL GOALS ARE SCORED FROM SET PIECES** SUCH AS THROW-INS AND CORNERS. "

RULES ON SCORING

Goals cannot be scored directly from a throw-in. The rules concerning corners are ambiguous, however. FIFA regulations state that "a corner-kick falls under the same guidelines as a direct free-kick," implying that such goals are legitimate.

Keep your hands evenly spaced on the ball

Your arms should follow the path of the ball

Launch angle is usually about 30 degrees

A short run-up provides momentum

Both your feet must stay on the ground

1 Hold the ball fully behind your head with both your hands. You are permitted to make a short run-up.

2 Bring your arms over your head and whip your body forward as you release the ball. This generates the power for the throw.

Corner-kicks

As with free-kicks (see pp.110–13), there are several options open to a player taking a corner. Aside from the inswinging and outswinging corners, there are five key variations.

Five corner styles

A corner represents a good opportunity to score a goal, so teams always work on these set piece routines. The following corner techniques are all practiced during training sessions: penalty spot, near post, far post, long, and short.

PENALTY SPOT CORNER
A corner aimed at the penalty spot may lure the keeper from his goal. The ball must travel fast to reach a teammate before it is intercepted.

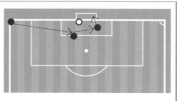

NEAR POST CORNER
The corner is aimed at the near goalpost so that it can be flicked on by a teammate to alter the ball's path and confuse the defenders.

FAR POST CORNER
Usually delivered as an outswinger, the ball will be curving toward the teammate attacking it, helping him to get power into his header.

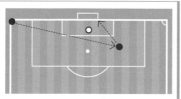

LONG CORNER
Used when the corner-taker notices a teammate hovering unmarked outside the six-yard box. A quick pass can set up a strike on goal.

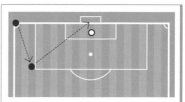

SHORT CORNER
A short-range pass to a teammate creates a different crossing or shooting angle. Defenders have no time to readjust themselves.

❝ CORNERS REPRESENT A GOOD OPPORTUNITY TO SCORE A GOAL. ❞

Taking a corner

The rules of taking a corner are simple: you are allowed to place the ball anywhere within the segment (the quarter circle between the goal line and the sideline) and you are not permitted to remove the corner flag. For more detailed techniques on taking a corner, see "Passing" (pp.76–79) and "Free-kicks" (pp.110–13).

Keep your head still and your eyes focused on the ball

BALL POSITIONING
❶ Take a corner from the left-hand side if you are right-footed.
❷ Take a corner from the right-hand side if you are left-footed.

Plant your non-striking foot firmly next to the ball

1 Place the ball anywhere in the segment, and take a step back. Pick a target (a teammate in the penalty area) and take a short run-up.

THE OLIMPICO

A goal scored directly from a corner with a curving shot is known as an "Olimpico" in South America. It is named in honor of Cesáreo Onzari of Uruguay, who scored against Argentina in this manner in 1924 when his team were the reigning Olympic champions.

Connect with the ball before the ground

2 Connect with the bottom of the ball on the right- or left-hand side, depending on the intended curve, if any, and follow through.

Free-kicks

All free-kicks are awarded against the team that has committed some infringement. There are various options open to you when you take the free-kick. You can strike the ball directly at the goal with force, or you can chip, curve, or pass to a teammate. Anything, in fact, that catches the opposing team unawares.

Types of free-kick

There are two types of free-kick—direct and indirect. Many direct free-kicks that are taken from the edge of the opposition penalty area represent good goalscoring opportunities, while most indirect free-kicks (except those taken from inside the penalty area) are little more than a means of restarting play.

DIRECT FREE-KICK

A direct free-kick is awarded against a team for committing a penalty foul, such as kicking a player instead of the ball, pushing, tripping, and similar infringements. If the referee deems the foul to be too malicious or dangerous, he will issue a yellow or red card. Direct free-kicks can be struck directly into the goal without the need for another teammate to touch the ball. The most punitive direct free-kick a team can face is a kick from the penalty spot (see pp.114–17).

INDIRECT FREE-KICK

An indirect free-kick is awarded against a team for committing a foul other than a penalty foul (for example, dangerous play) or for infringing certain technical requirements of the laws (for example, offside). An indirect free-kick requires the ball to be touched by more than one player on the same team before it can enter the goal.

HOW TO TELL THE DIFFERENCE

If in doubt about whether a free-kick is direct or indirect, watch the referee. He indicates a direct kick with an outstretched arm (horizontal) and an indirect with a vertical arm position.

DIRECT FREE-KICK   INDIRECT FREE-KICK

Approach the ball from an angle of about 45 degrees

Make sure the last stride before impact is a long one

The curving free-kick

If the free-kick is awarded close to the goal, the defending team will build a defensive wall (see p.162). When taking the free-kick, if you give the ball enough curve, it will bend around the wall and also make it difficult for the keeper to judge its flight. The principles of getting the ball to curve are the same whether the kick is taken from a dead ball situation or on the move (see p.97).

WHERE TO STRIKE THE BALL

THE QUICK FREE-KICK

Usually, when you stand over a free-kick, you must wait for the referee's whistle before starting play. But you are permitted to ask the referee if you can take a "quick" kick without the whistle signal, to try to gain an advantage.

" MANY DIRECT FREE-KICKS THAT ARE TAKEN FROM THE EDGE OF THE OPPOSITION PENALTY AREA **REPRESENT GOOD GOALSCORING OPPORTUNITIES**. **"**

Plant your standing leg firmly on the ground

Wrap your instep around the bottom right section of the ball to generate spin

Free-kick options

Sometimes the success of a free-kick is down to the skill and ingenuity of one player; on other occasions it is a team effort. Free-kicks are good opportunities to score the goals that win matches, so coaches work on them extensively with players during training.

KEY	
O	Goalkeeper
●	Attacker
●	Defender
-----	Ball motion
—	Player motion

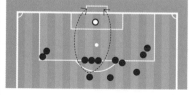

CURVING SHOT

The art of bending a shot around the defensive wall and away from the dive of the keeper. Curved shots are created by striking the ball on its side and generating spin (see p.79).

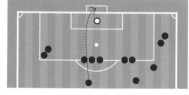

DIPPING SHOT

A challenging skill that requires you to strike the ball over the wall rather than around it; if struck correctly, the dipping ball drops at the end of its flight.

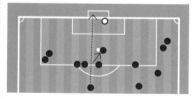

THROUGH THE WALL

You have to strike the ball low so it goes under the players in the wall as they jump; or strike directly at a teammate in the wall who jumps out of the way to create a space.

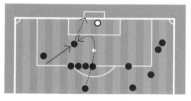

CHIP INTO SPACE

You should dink the ball into an area 8–10yd (7–9m) from the goal, where the goalkeeper cannot easily claim it; the intention is that one of your teammates is then able to shoot or head at goal.

BECKHAM'S CURVED FREE-KICK

The ball leaves Beckham's foot at 80mph (130kph)

At this stage, the ball is flying slightly to the right from Beckham's perspective, fooling the goalkeeper into making a small move to the left

The ball has now started to change direction. It swerves above and to the side of the Greek player on the left of the defensive wall

30yd

Bend it like Beckham

In 2001, David Beckham stepped up to take a free-kick in the 93rd minute of a match against Greece knowing that he had to score to secure England's qualification for the following year's World Cup finals. Sure enough, he hit an unstoppable curving shot from 30 yd (28m), leaving the Greek keeper helpless. The ball hit the top corner of the net traveling at 42mph (68kph). It swerved approximately 9ft (3m) during its flight.

DAVID BECKHAM

The most famous soccer player of his generation, London-born David Beckham has played for his country more than 100 times. Blessed with one of the most prized right feet in the game, Beckham has mastered the art of the whipped-in cross and free-kick techniques during his spells at Manchester United, Real Madrid, LA Galaxy, and AC Milan.

KEY

- O Greek keeper
- O England
- ● Greece
- ----- Ball motion

The kick was taken almost directly in line with the center of the goal

BECKHAM

The ball is now at its maximum height, curving viciously

It dips into the top left hand corner with the keeper stranded

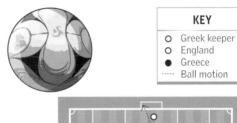

Penalties

Penalties are awarded for fouls committed in the penalty area, such as tripping and pushing. They are taken from the penalty spot, which is located directly between the goalposts, 12yd (11m) from the goal line. Scoring from penalties requires composure and skillful ball placement, saving penalties requires agility and anticipation. Goalkeepers are rarely expected to save penalties.

Penalty shootouts

Draws are acceptable in some matches (almost all league games), but not in matches where a winner has to be found in order for a tournament to progress or reach a conclusion (cup ties, cup finals, and play-offs). Penalty shootouts are a way of forcing a result when the scores are level at the end of such a game, usually after a period of extra-time.

WOBBLY KNEES

In the 1984 European Cup final penalty shootout, Liverpool goalkeeper Bruce Grobbelaar wobbled his legs in mock terror, causing two AS Roma players to miss. Liverpool won the trophy.

Penalty rules

The penalty is not just a battle of wits between the taker and the keeper, there are various rules and restrictions to be adhered to for other players, too.

EXCLUSION ZONE
All players barring the taker and the goalkeeper must stay outside the penalty area

- Defender
- Attacker
- ○ Goalkeeper
- Referee

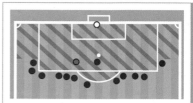

The keeper will usually calculate that his best chance of saving the kick is to dive early to one side

6yd (5.5m)

FINDING A WINNER

Shootouts were introduced by UEFA in 1970 and FIFA in 1976. Each team takes five penalties against the other, with the kicks alternating. The team that's ahead at the end wins the match. If the scores are still level, the match goes into "sudden death." The first team to fall behind when an equal number of penalties has been taken by each side loses. Penalty shootouts are often considered an unsatisfactory way of deciding matches, but no better alternative has yet been found.

PENALTY DO'S AND DON'TS	
DO	DON'T
Keep your weight over the ball	Take too long a run-up
Make a plan and stick to it	Let the keeper psyche you out
Fool the keeper with your eyes	Hit the ball at chest height ...
Strike the ball firmly	... or too close to the keeper

❝ A SOCCER MATCH GOES INTO 'SUDDEN DEATH' IF THE SCORES ARE STILL LEVEL AFTER A PENALTY SHOOTOUT. ❞

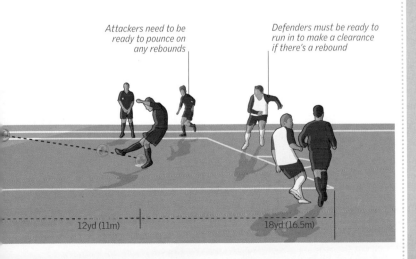

Attackers need to be ready to pounce on any rebounds

Defenders must be ready to run in to make a clearance if there's a rebound

12yd (11m)   18yd (16.5m)

Where to shoot

Success or failure with the penalty-kick is partly determined by the strength of the shot, but if a penalty is poorly placed the goalkeeper may reach it. So where should you aim for to guarantee the greatest chance of success?

KEY

Goalkeeper will save unless he overcommits

Goalkeeper may save if shot is struck weakly

Goalkeeper is highly unlikely to save

ALLESSANDRO DEL PIERO

The Juventus and Italy striker has a good penalty-taking record. He often uses delicate chips to outwit the keeper. He was brought on near the end of the 2006 World Cup final against France to take a penalty, and he scored.

❝ A PENALTY THAT IS STRUCK FIRMLY INTO THE BOTTOM OR TOP CORNER WILL REGISTER A GOAL, BUT THERE IS VERY **LITTLE MARGIN FOR ERROR**. ❞

Types of penalty

You have three options when taking a spot kick: attempt to pass the ball into the net, try a cheeky chip, or strike the ball firmly. A penalty struck firmly into the bottom or top corner will register a goal but there is little margin for error; you cannot kick the ball wide.

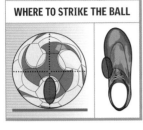

PENALTY PASS
When you place a penalty, you effectively pass the ball into the net. This provides accuracy and is a good option if the keeper has dived early.

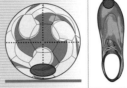

PENALTY CHIP
This is the most audacious kind of penalty, but extremely risky. You have to rely on the goalkeeper diving before you make the strike.

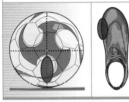

POWER SHOT
You sacrifice accuracy for speed with this option and stand a good chance of success if you don't blast the ball wide or high.

PIRES' POOR PENALTY

In October 2005, Arsenal was awarded a penalty in a match against Manchester City. Instead of shooting, Robert Pires opted for the unorthodox but perfectly legal option of knocking the ball for Thierry Henry to strike. However, Pires' touch was so feeble that the ball failed to move and a defender cleared it.

❝ THE PENALTY CHIP IS THE MOST AUDACIOUS KIND OF PENALTY. YOU HAVE TO RELY ON THE GOALKEEPER DIVING BEFORE YOU MAKE THE STRIKE. ❞

Goalkeeping

Goalkeeping is so different from other soccer roles that it almost seems to belong to another sport. All players need agility, bravery, a strong physical presence, and good distribution and decisionmaking abilities, but goalkeepers have to have these characteristics in abundance. The three fundamentals that an aspiring goalkeeper needs to master are: stance (being "athletically primed"); body positioning (being aware of angles of attack and your position in relation to the goal); and shot-stopping.

Stance

You have to be continually alert to the possibility of a shot, leaning slightly forward so that your weight is on your toes rather than your heels. This places you in the optimum position to dive quickly or run toward an attacker if the situation demands it.

Body positioning

You should always know where you and the ball are relative to the goal. To avoid turning around to check, construct a mental image of the goal area. Imagine a capital "T" with the shaft running through the penalty spot and the cross stroke stretching between the posts.

Shot-stopping

The key task for any goalkeeper is knowing how to catch or stop the ball. There are two differing techniques for this depending on whether the ball is traveling along the ground or in the air—the "W" and the "M." Whenever possible, you should attempt to use both your hands when gathering the ball or making a save. Two hands together are stronger and cover more area than one.

When the ball is caught the thumbs should be almost touching

Bend the knees to "close the gate" and prevent the ball going through the legs

THE "W"
The basic hand position when dealing with a shot close to the body and above the waist forms the letter "W" with the thumbs touching and the fingers pointing upward—a good position to catch the ball.

THE "M"
When dealing with a ball that reaches you below waist height and close to the body, you should form a downward pointing "M" with your hands, with the four fingers in the middle squeezed together and the thumbs pointing out.

Narrowing the angle

As a goalkeeper, the nearer you are to an attacker running toward you with the ball, the less chance he has of seeing the goal clearly. This method is known as "narrowing the angle." When an attacker is running toward the goal with the ball or charging onto a through pass, you need to decide instantly whether to stay back or run forward. You don't want to be caught in no man's land, where you have run away from the goal but are still not close enough to the ball to prevent or block a shot.

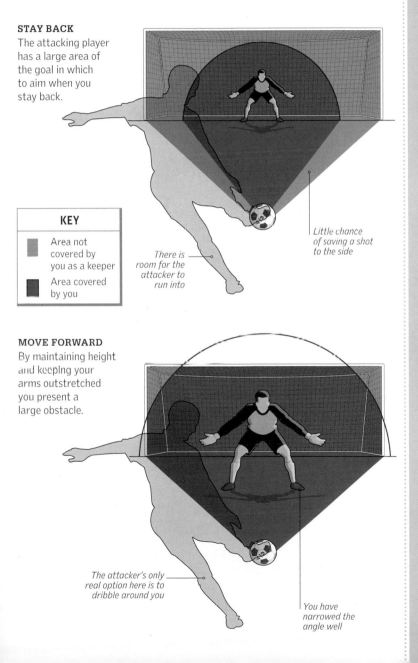

STAY BACK
The attacking player has a large area of the goal in which to aim when you stay back.

KEY

■ Area not covered by you as a keeper

■ Area covered by you

There is room for the attacker to run into

Little chance of saving a shot to the side

MOVE FORWARD
By maintaining height and keeping your arms outstretched you present a large obstacle.

The attacker's only real option here is to dribble around you

You have narrowed the angle well

Grounding

When you catch a ball but have no chance of staying on your feet, you need to ground the ball as soon as possible to bring it under control and keep from spilling it into the path of incoming attackers.

Prepare your hands for the catch

1 Dive with your hands in the "W" position, watching the ball closely as it approaches.

Keep your torso fairly rigid during the dive

2 As you hit the ground, land on one knee with the other leg outstretched. Catch the ball slightly above its center.

Focus all your upper body weight down onto the ball

3 Bring the ball firmly down to the ground, holding it tightly, with the hands still in the "W" position.

Diving save

The diving save is the most spectacular in a goalkeeper's repertoire. The keys to achieving this successfully are quick reactions, good footwork, and getting into position early.

Launch your body toward the ball

1 Bend the leg closest to the ball and watch its flight. Spring to the side with one arm outstretched and the wrist held firm.

Watch the ball closely to ensure you judge the distance

Get your fingertips to the ball

2 Push the ball away from the goal to prevent attackers from capitalizing on a rebound, then brace yourself for landing.

> ❝ **THE KEYS TO A SUCCESSFUL DIVING SAVE** ARE **QUICK REACTIONS, GOOD FOOTWORK,** AND GETTING INTO **POSITION EARLY.** ❞

A WORD IN YOUR EAR

In the Belgian league in January 2004, Racing Genk's Jan Moons became the first goalkeeper to receive instructions from the bench via an earpiece. His side beat FC Bruges 1–0.

Goalkeeper's roles

Being a good goalkeeper isn't all about eye-catching saves and a strong physical presence. As a keeper, you have a duty to start attacks by distributing the ball well and being the unofficial captain of the team's defense.

DISTRIBUTION DISTANCES

You need to tailor your distribution method to the player you are trying to reach. Often your target will be on the other side of the halfway line, which will usually necessitate a long punt or a half-volley (see opposite).

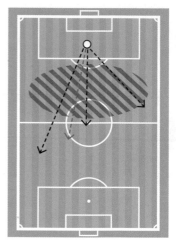

KEY	
– – Punt	– – Roll out
– – Half-volley	O Goalkeeper
– – Long throw	⧗ Danger area

LEV YASHIN

The only keeper to be voted European Player of the Year, Yashin played for Dynamo Moscow. He represented the USSR at three World Cups and was known as "The Black Spider" because he played as though he had eight arms.

Distribution

If you catch or pick up the ball while keeping, you have exactly six seconds to put the ball down again and restart play, otherwise you can be penalized. Your goal should be to launch a speedy counterattack, so look up quickly to find a free teammate. There are four methods you can use to start a new attack, each with its own merits.

Connect cleanly with the middle part of your foot

Good timing is paramount with this technique

THE PUNT
Drop the ball from your hands and volley it. It is possible to cover long distances with this technique.

THE HALF-VOLLEY
This is similar to the punt, but here you let the ball hit the ground a fraction of a second before making contact.

Technique is similar to a bowler's action in cricket

Technique is similar to 10-pin bowling

THE OVERARM THROW
Grip the ball tightly, then move your throwing arm around in an arc over your shoulder to launch the ball upfield.

THE ROLL OUT
Rolling the ball out is a good option over short to medium distances and is extremely accurate.

Catch or punch?

While goalkeeping, you have to decide whether to deal with high
balls played into the penalty area by catching them, punching
them, or staying on your goal line. You should only do the latter
if you believe you stand a poor chance of getting to the ball first.

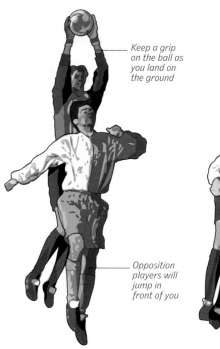

*Keep a grip
on the ball as
you land on
the ground*

*A strong
punch gets
the ball
out of the
danger area*

*Opposition
players will
jump in
front of you*

*You have
a height
advantage
by virtue of
being able
to use
your arms*

CATCHING THE BALL
Your best option is to catch the ball,
since this will end the attack. However,
you have to reach the ball unimpeded.

PUNCHING THE BALL
The next best option is to punch the ball.
Try to use both your arms although you
may be able to get only one to the ball.

Dealing with crosses

The task of catching a cross or corner is ostensibly a simple one—follow the
flight of the ball clearly and time the jump. Complications arise, however, with
the number of players in the penalty
area. You must shout loudly to indicate
your intentions to the defenders. Also,
you must be strong enough to compete
with the opposition's attackers.

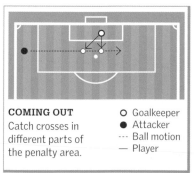

DEFENDING A CROSS
The secret of defending a cross is all
about organization. Defenders need to
pick up the players they are supposed
to be marking and you need to be
authoritative as a keeper.

COMING OUT
Catch crosses in
different parts of
the penalty area.

○ Goalkeeper
● Attacker
--- Ball motion
— Player

Marshaling the defense

Being a goalkeeper, you are the only player able to see the whole game in front of you. You are best placed to organize defenses for the general benefit of the team.

Under orders

A quiet keeper is not doing his job properly. You should be extremely vocal in warning your teammates when an opponent is unmarked, and in announcing your intention to clear or catch a ball. You should bark orders at your defense when setting up defensive walls, as you alone know where they should stand to give you the best chance of saving a shot.

> **"** A KEEPER SHOULD BE **EXTREMELY VOCAL** IN **WARNING HIS TEAMMATES** WHEN AN OPPONENT IS UNMARKED. **"**

PETER SCHMEICHEL

The Denmark and Manchester United keeper was a huge physical presence on the field. He is 6ft 4in (1.93m) and wears size XXXL shoes.

GOALKEEPING MOMENTS

THE SCORPION KICK

Former Colombian keeper René Higuita performed the "Scorpion kick," bouncing forward onto his hands, arching his back, and kicking the ball away with his heels.

TRAUTMANN'S NECK

Germany's Bert Trautmann came to England as a prisoner of war. He signed for Manchester City in 1949. He played most of the 1956 FA Cup Final with a broken neck.

A GUST OF WIND

Tottenham Hotspur's Pat Jennings scored a famous goalkeeping goal in the 1967 Charity Shield. His clearance was caught by wind and sailed past Manchester United's Alex Stepney.

Tackling

Tackling is hugely important—it's the principal means of wresting possession from the opposition. It is a skill that every member of a team, including forwards, needs to be prepared to use, coining the phrase "defending from the front."

Types of tackle

There are several kinds of tackle, each requiring different techniques, but two principles apply to them all. The first is timing: as a good tackler, you should know exactly when to attempt to win the ball. You are likely to miss the ball altogether if you lunge in prematurely. The second is safety, not only in terms of avoiding injury but also in making sure that a clumsy tackle doesn't lead to a free-kick.

Poke tackle

Stay on your feet and poke or prod the ball away from your opponent into the path of a teammate. It is best used when the ball has bounced up between knee and waist height.

Wait for the ball to drop before making your move

1 Get yourself as close as possible to your opponent before making the tackle and wait for the ball to come into view.

2 Time yourself carefully and flick your foot out and through your opponent's legs to poke the ball away.

Player in possession is often unaware that you are about to make the challenge

Aim for the gap between the player's legs

Block tackle

The block tackle is made when a defending player meets an attacker head on. Both players use the inside of their tackling foot, forceably making contact with the ball. Both players stay on their feet. The block tackle is used more often than any other kind of tackle.

1 Before you make your challenge, "jockey" your opponent. This involves standing in front of the opponent and denying him room.

Use your back leg as a pivot to move sideways during jockeying

Move your weight forward into the tackle

Keep your ankle firm throughout the tackle

2 When the opponent draws his leg back to kick the ball, bring your tackling foot toward the ball.

3 Once the tackle is engaged, you still have to work hard to control the ball and win possession.

LUNGING IN PREMATURELY IS LIKELY TO RESULT IN YOU **MISSING THE BALL** ALTOGETHER.

Slide tackle

Both dramatic and emphatic, you should use this technique only when there are no alternatives. This is because you will always end up on the ground and invariably out of the game.

1 Approaching from the side, make your tackle with the leg farthest forward. Bend your other leg to allow yourself to slide in.

Stay on your feet until the last possible moment

2 Knock the ball away, ideally to a teammate. Get back on your feet as soon as possible after making the tackle.

The player in possession will fall over your legs

Slide on the knee of your non-striking leg

MOORE STOPS BRAZIL

One of the most famous and elegant tackles in history was made during the "Clash of the Champions"—England's encounter with Brazil in the group stages of the 1970 World Cup in Mexico. As Brazil's Jairzinho dribbled menacingly into the box, Bobby Moore slid in with an immaculate tackle. Technically, he used his "wrong" foot (the one farther upfield) but he rose majestically and carried the ball out of defense as if the challenge had been merely routine.

The "hook" tackle

This is a variation of the slide tackle in which you "hook" your foot around the ball. You begin behind the player in possession at an angle of about 45 degrees. Challenge him, and hook your foot around the ball and steal possession. Then pass to a teammate.

The attacking player stumbles over the challenge

Use your arm to support your body on the ground

Recovery tackle

Similar in many ways to the sliding tackle, the recovery tackle is not intended to gain possession or set up a pass to a teammate. It's usually made when an attacker has the ball near the sideline and needs to be stopped from advancing. Your best option is to kick the ball into touch.

Get your body in front of the player in possession

Slide in and kick the ball into touch

OUT OF PLAY
The recovery tackle is used to dispossess an opponent and put the ball out of play.

● Defender
● Attacker
--- Ball motion
— Player motion

❝ EXECUTE **THE RECOVERY TACKLE** WHEN **THE ATTACKER** NEEDS TO BE **STOPPED FROM ADVANCING**. ❞

Freestyle skills

Freestyle soccer is essentially juggling with a ball in as creative a fashion as possible. As in the real game, any part of the body can be used except the hands and the arms. Although most of the skills associated with freestyle soccer are not directly relevant to match play, they are worth mastering as they develop ball control and encourage creativity and improvisation.

The moves

There are many different moves that an aspiring freestyler can learn and, as with other freestyle sports (such as skateboarding), new tricks are constantly being invented. Tricks usually fall into three main categories: juggling (keeping the ball airborne), flick-ups, and catches.

Keepy-uppie

In the simplest form, you have to keep the ball from touching the ground for as long as possible, usually with the feet and head. A fundamental skill, keepy-uppie is also known as juggling.

Head stall

In this trick, you have to balance the ball on your forehead. Keep your eyes on the ball while performing and make small neck and body adjustments to keep it in place.

Watch the ball closely at all times

Small and subtle foot movements work best

Readjust your neck to make your head as flat as possible

Remain agile and light on your feet

❝ TRICKS USUALLY FALL INTO THREE MAIN CATEGORIES: JUGGLING, FLICK-UPS, AND CATCHES. ❞

The rainbow

In this trick, you have to flick the ball behind you and then back-heel it over your head before bringing it under control at the front of your body. The flight of the ball forms an arc over your head, hence the trick's name.

Trap the ball between your heel and toes

1 Place your weaker foot in front of the ball, touching the heel. Roll the ball a short distance up the back of your ankle with your other foot.

Drive your heel up and through to propel the ball

2 When the ball is just above your heel, hop forward, leading with your stronger foot, and flick up the ball over your head with the weaker one.

Follow the flight of the ball carefully

3 Concentration and skill is required to anticipate the path of the ball over your head and onto your feet. Then start juggling.

SOCCER AND CAPOEIRA

Young, urban South Americans have developed a soccer version of Capoeira, the Afro-Brazilian dance-based martial art.

❝ TO PERFORM THE RAINBOW, FLICK THE BALL BEHIND YOU, THEN BACK-HEEL IT OVER YOUR HEAD BEFORE BRINGING IT UNDER CONTROL IN FRONT OF YOUR BODY. ❞

Around the world

In this trick, you have to kick the ball up in the air during a keepy-uppie session and circle your kicking foot around it before it begins to drop. This must be done smoothly enough to get your foot back in position to continue the juggling at the end of the maneuver. The kicking foot can go around the ball either on the outside (away from the center of your body) or on the inside.

Keep your head still throughout the trick

Stretch out your arms to maintain balance

Strike with a bit more force than usual

Keep your foot away from the ball

1 Start by juggling as normal, keeping the ball under close control, then begin the trick by kicking the ball higher than usual.

2 As the ball rises, circle your foot over the ball, then control it and continue juggling as it drops.

MAJOR FREESTYLE TOURNAMENTS

The rules may not have been standardized, and the sport may lack an official governing body, but there have been several self-proclaimed freestyle world championships over the years.

MASTERS OF THE GAME I

An organization called "Masters of the Game" held a tournament at the Amsterdam Arena, Netherlands, in 2003. It was won by South Korea's Mr. Woo.

MASTERS OF THE GAME II

The second Masters of the Game world championship was held in 2006 and was won by the UK's John Farnworth.

KOMBALL KONTEST

The Komball Kontest held in France in 2008 introduced a new format for freestyle competitions. Sixteen participants performed individually in front of three judges, with the best eight progressing to a knockout phase. Ireland's Nam "the Man" Ngueyen was crowned European soccer freestyle champion.

RED BULL STREET STYLE

In 2008, the Red Bull Street Style world finals were held in São Paulo, Brazil. A panel judged the participants on ball control, technique, style, and their ability to synchronize their movements with background music.

Unofficial world championships

Although the sport is not yet organized by a universally recognized international body, several self-proclaimed freestyle world championships have taken place. They have spawned numerous freestyle stars, such as Mr. Woo, John Farnworth, Nam the Man, and Arnaud Garnier.

> **FREESTYLE PERFORMERS** ARE MARKED ON THE **VARIETY** AND **DIFFICULTY OF TRICKS** PERFORMED.

MILENE DOMINGUES

Known as Ronaldinha, the ex-wife of Brazilian star Ronaldo is one of the best female players in Europe. With 55,198 touches, she holds the women's record for ball-juggling.

THE JUDGES' BRIEF

According to the World Freestyle Football Association (WFFA), established in 2005, performers should be given scores out of 10 in the following categories:

- Control: demonstrating and maintaining ball control using various parts of the body.
- Transitions: moving fluidly from one trick to the next.
- Use of both feet.
- Use of the entire body, except hands.
- Combinations: including consistently completing the same move twice or more.
- Sticks: stalling the ball on different parts of the body.
- Variety of tricks.
- Level of difficulty.
- Creativity: originality and imagination shown in performance, using crowd reaction as a guide.
- Blotto: pushing the envelope of the sport to new levels.

Injuries

Soccer does not have the frequency of contact injuries sustained in rugby and football. However, players' twists and turns put huge stresses on their joints, and tackles and collisions at high speed can be serious. At the top level, injuries are inevitable but can still affect a side's season or even shape a soccer player's entire career.

Injury facts

The most common months for injuries are during pre-season training and the season's early months, when muscles are comparatively untrained. The most common moments in games to get injured are the two 15-minute periods at the end of both halves. Eighty percent of injuries are severe enough to rule players out of at least one match—the average number of matches missed is as high as four.

> **EIGHTY PERCENT** OF **INJURIES** ARE **SEVERE** ENOUGH TO **RULE PLAYERS OUT** OF AT LEAST **ONE MATCH**.

Rehabilitation

When top players get injured, they have a team of medical experts to guide them through the painful process of rehabilitation. In the case of a broken leg, after approximately four weeks in a cast, the player will begin a grueling session of gym work, focused on rebuilding the muscle tissue. Usually the injured body part ends up stronger than it was before the injury.

COMMON SOCCER INJURIES	
AREA OF BODY	**INJURY/DESCRIPTION**
HEAD	CUTS—general abrasions suffered in the course of play CONCUSSION—result of an impact to the head
BACK	MUSCLE STRAIN—caused by excessive spinal stretching SLIPPED DISK—the pain of a vertebrae pushing on a nerve
ARMS	FRACTURE—usually as a result of an awkward fall DISLOCATION—whereby a bone is dislodged from its socket
LEGS (UPPER)	GROIN STRAIN—overstretching of the groin muscles DEAD LEG—loss of feeling of movement from hard blow HAMSTRING STRAIN OR TEAR—usually incurred while running at high speed
KNEES	CRUCIATE LIGAMENT DAMAGE—overbending or rotation of the knee TORN CARTILAGE—damage to the knee's shock absorbers
LEGS (LOWER)	CALF STRAIN—overstretching of the lower leg SHIN SPLINTS—hard impact to the shin
ANKLES AND FEET	TWISTED OR BROKEN ANKLE—caused by rapid turning or a bad tackle ACHILLES STRAIN—strained tendon in the heel METATARSAL FRACTURE—fractured foot bones

" THE MOST COMMON MONTHS FOR INJURIES ARE DURING **PRE-SEASON TRAINING** AND **THE SEASON'S EARLY MONTHS**. "

DJIBRIL CISSÉ

Djibril Cissé had only played 19 games for Liverpool when in October 2004 a tackle from Blackburn Rovers' Jay McEveley broke two bones in his leg. Then, playing for France against China on June 7, 2006, he suffered another broken leg.

Teamwork

Teamwork: key concepts

There are many commonly used strategies in soccer, but certain principles can be applied to them all. Every player needs to have a grasp of these fundamentals if they are to succeed on the field. For a lucky few, it is a process that comes instinctively; for everyone else, a little theory, coupled with plenty of hard work on the training ground, is invaluable.

The team is everything

There is no "I" in "team." Individual brilliance is useless unless it is harnessed for the good of the team. A player needs to bear five things in mind on the field: find space so that teammates can pass to him; offer his teammates support whenever they are on the ball; guard possession of the ball; move to a new position after he has made a pass; and keep teammates informed of his intentions.

SUPPORT

Players must support their colleagues by joining them in attack, running back to help out in defense, or filling in for a teammate who has left his playing position after joining an attack. Forwards must follow up shots looking for rebounds off the goalkeeper.

COMMUNICATION

Communication on the field is vital. A player in possession of the ball isn't always aware of his teammates' intentions. Therefore, it is essential they let him know where they are, where they are heading, and where they want the ball to be played. This can be done by using one of a number of calls.

ROY KEANE

A midfielder, Roy Keane was an ultimate team player during his distinguished career with Nottingham Forest, Manchester United, Celtic, and the Republic of Ireland.

vodafone

Use of space

When children play soccer, they all tend to follow the ball. Then they realize they will be more useful to their team if they get away from the pack and find some space. The history of soccer can be seen as a process of gradual enlightenment when it comes to space; today, it is given the importance it deserves.

Pass and move

The pass-and-move philosophy is based on the idea that if a player is static it is easy for opponents to pick him up. The great Liverpool teams of the 1970s and early '80s were masters of pass-and-move soccer, exhausting opponents and keeping possession with constantly shifting triangles.

Possession

In soccer, possession is nine-tenths of the law. Barring own-goals, no one can score against you if they don't have the ball. Chasing the play also tires and frustrates opponents. Possession soccer has developed into a full-fledged tactic, and one that is related to the "pass-and-move" philosophy (see left).

PERPETUAL MOTION

The pass-and-move philosophy is based on the idea that if players are constantly on the move, they are more difficult to mark.

After passing, the player moves into space ready to receive a return pass from his teammate

A player passes the ball to his unmarked teammate

POSSESSION IS NINE-TENTHS OF THE LAW. BARRING OWN-GOALS, NO ONE CAN SCORE AGAINST YOU IF THEY DON'T HAVE THE BALL.

Global styles

The way soccer should be played is a much-discussed topic, and the answer given varies from country to country. The descriptions below are generalizations, but they certainly have some validity.

Central America
Mexico (1986): Crashed out of the World Cup on penalties without losing a game

Latin
Brazil (1970): Considered the greatest team in World Cup history

> **❝ ATTACKS** BY THE BRITISH ARE **SET UP QUICKLY WITH FEW TOUCHES** ON THE BALL. THE GAME PLAN FOR THEIR STYLE OF PLAY IS **BASED ON SUBSTANCE OVER STYLE**. ❞

CENTRAL AMERICAN

Players (type): Clever, but sometimes excessive, dribblers
Characteristics: Ball tends to be moved around the field in a series of short passes; all players have good one-on-one skills; tempo of matches is often slow
Success: Mexico is the primary representative of this style

LATIN

Players (type): Confident with the ball, good dribblers, and creative
Characteristics: The Latin game style has a possession-oriented character suited to the hot, draining climates in which matches are typically played
Success: Portugal, Argentina, Spain, and Brazil are among the world's best

Continental
Holland (1974): Thrilled the world with its brand of Total Soccer (see p.149)

British
England (1966): Won the World Cup with a mix of skill, grit, and determination

Northern European
West Germany (1974): Stopped Total Soccer in its tracks in the World Cup final

Italian
Italy (2006): A World Cup-winning mix of defensive stability and attacking flair

African
Cameroon (1990): The first African side to progress to the World Cup quarter-finals

CONTINENTAL

Players (type): A combination of the Latin and Northern European games
Characteristics: All players are comfortable on the ball; the emphasis is on creativity combined with composure and coordination among the players
Success: Holland and France are the style's leading representatives

BRITISH

Players (type): Physical, athletic, fast tempo, and direct
Characteristics: Attacks are set up quickly with few touches on the ball; the game plan for the British style of play is based on substance over style
Success: Success at club level; not on the world stage for the national team

NORTHERN EUROPEAN

Players (type): Hardworking, aggressive, organized, and swift
Characteristics: Direct game with forceful, although sometimes highly predictable, attacks; their defenses are typically hard to break down
Success: Germany remains the standard-bearer for this style

ITALIAN

Players (type): Skillful, inventive, and cautious
Characteristics: Reluctance to commit too many players forwards in attack due to great emphasis on defense
Success: Italian clubs feature in the latter stages of major European titles; the national side is a regular contender at major championships

AFRICAN

Players (type): Athletic and physical
Characteristics: Touch-and-move soccer similar to the Latin style; there is emphasis on stylish attacking soccer and displays of individual skill
Success: African teams continue to threaten to reach the latter stages of the World Cup

Formations

The formation of a team is determined by the positions allocated to players and their relationship to each other. Managers select formations with two main goals: to neutralize the opposition, and to exploit its weaknesses. Formations are listed in numbers, with the defenders listed first and the strikers listed last (goalkeepers are never listed).

Early formations

The earliest formations were mostly attack-based but became more balanced as they evolved. The following are some of the most influential formations in soccer's formative years.

> ❝ **FORMATIONS** ARE MEANT TO **NEUTRALIZE** THE OPPOSITION AND **EXPLOIT ITS WEAKNESSES**. ❞

1-2-7
In the early days, forward passes were not permitted. Players could pass the ball sideways or backward, although this was seen as contrary to the spirit of the game. Instead, players moved up the field together using a kind of charge-dribble.

The emphasis of a 1-2-7 was on relentless attack

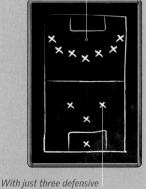

With just three defensive players, cover at the back was minimal

DEVELOPMENT OF FORMATIONS

The way teams have lined up on a field has changed radically throughout the game's history.

1867 Offside rule first introduced

1872 Royal Engineers win the FA Cup with a 1-2-7 formation

1889 Preston North End win the English league and FA Cup playing a 2-3-5

1925 Changes in the offside rule give birth to the W-M

1934 Vittorio Pozzo's Italy wins the World Cup with a 2-3-2-3

1860 1870 1880 1900 1920 1930 1940

THE DIAGONAL

During the 1940s, Brazil manager Flávio Costa developed a curiously lopsided system known as the diagonal. It was similar to the W-M, except that the two left-sided midfielders were stationed farther forward than their equivalents on the right. Costa enjoyed considerable success with the system, but abandoned it halfway through the 1950 World Cup campaign in favor of a conventional W-M. Many blamed his decision for Brazil's sensational loss to Uruguay in the final match that cost Brazil the trophy. The defeat is considered the darkest day in Brazilian sports history.

2-3-5

In 1866, the rules were changed to allow forward passing (provided there were at least three opponents between the player receiving the ball and the goal). Due to this extra pressure on defenses, by the 1880s the more defensive 2-3-5 (the pyramid) had evolved.

3-2-2-3 (W-M)

The offside rule (see pp.18–19) was amended in 1925 to encourage more attacking soccer. A player receiving the ball was now onside provided there were two opponents ahead of him. To deal with the increased attacking threat, the 3-2-2-3 (or W-M) was developed.

Five forwards gave teams ample scope in attack

Center halves were responsible for breaking down play and instigating attacks

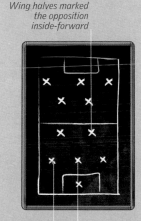

Wing halves marked the opposition inside-forward

Fullbacks mark the opposition wingers

The center back marks the opposing center-forward

1953 *Hungary exposes the weaknesses in the W-M by playing the M-U*

1958 *Brazil wins the World Cup with 4-2-4*

1966 *England's "wingless wonders" win the World Cup with a midfield diamond*

1970 *Ajax wins the first European Cup*

1990 *AC Milan deploys the definitive modern 4-4-2*

2009 *The dominant contemporary formations are fluid variants of 4-5-1 and 4-2-3-1, even 4-6-0*

1950   1960   1970   1980 1990   2000   2010

THE **4-2-4 FORMATION** WAS DEVELOPED TO **REINFORCE THE DEFENSE** WITHOUT SACRIFICING ATTACKING PLAY.

3-2-3-2 (M-U)
In November 1953, Hungary (the Olympic soccer champion) lined up against England at Wembley in a revolutionary M-U formation. The team gave its host, who was playing a rigid W-M, a soccer lesson, and went on to win the match 6–3.

A deep-lying center forward pulled the man-marking center back out of position

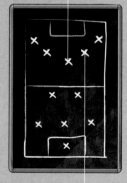

The withdrawal of the center forward left space for the inside- forward to run into

4-2-4
Developed to reinforce the defense without sacrificing attacking play, the 4-2-4 exploded onto the international scene with Brazil's victory at the 1958 World Cup. It operates as a 3-3-4 when in possession and a 4-3-3 in defense.

One of the forwards drops back into midfield to help out when necessary

One of the fullbacks advances to join the midfield in attack; the other helps in defense

Other formations

Several theories on how to play the game abounded throughout Europe in the 1920s and '30s—the following are among the most famous of those systems.

Danubian school
A modification of the 2-3-5 formation, utilized by the Austrians, Czechs, and Hungarians in the 1920s, it relied on short passing and individual skills. It reached its peak in the early 1930s.

Il metodo ("The method")
Devised by Vittorio Pozzo, coach of the Italian national side in the 1930s, *il metodo* involved pulling back two of the forwards to just in front of midfield to create a 2-3-2-3 formation.

Modern formations

During the first 100 years of soccer's existence, only a handful of formations were regularly used. There also tended to be just one used in a given era. Since the 1960s, the tactical side of the game has been blown wide open. Flexibility has become the watchword, with the team increasingly tailored to the opposition and to the way a match is panning out.

4-4-2

The basic modern formation, the 4-4-2, places a burden on midfielders: one of the central pair must go up and support attacks, while the other drops back. Wide players help out in defense and attack, creating a temporary 4-2-4. The two strikers work in tandem and need to have a good understanding of each other.

One striker can drop deep to create a 4-4-1-1

Wide players provide cover in defense and extra options in attack

❝ THE BASIC MODERN FORMATION, THE 4-4-2, PLACES A BURDEN ON THE MIDFIELDERS. ❞

ARRIGO SACCHI

Although he never played professionally, Arrigo Sacchi managed the great AC Milan in the early 1990s. He perfected the 4-4-2, where he made his players move across the field as a packed unit

3-5-2/5-3-2

The difference between 3-5-2 and 5-3-2 is one of emphasis, with the former being more attack-oriented than the latter since it has more midfielders. In either variant, the key men are the wide players, usually described as wingers, who are expected to help out with both attack and defense.

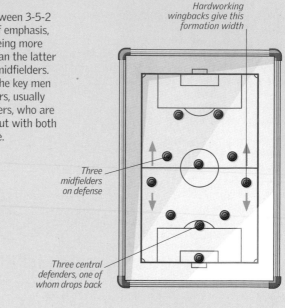

Hardworking wingbacks give this formation width

Three midfielders on defense

Three central defenders, one of whom drops back

4-3-3

Essentially a more defensive version of the 4-2-4, the 4-3-3 was first pioneered by Brazil at the 1962 World Cup. The three midfielders could be staggered in various ways and tended to move across the field as a unit. Few teams now start with this system, but many adopt it late on in a match if they're chasing a game.

Wingers can join the attack or drop into midfield to defend

In attack, two midfielders push forward with one dropping back to help the defense

4-5-1

This is essentially a defensive formation, with a packed midfield and a lone striker left to fend for himself, or hold the ball up, until support arrives, usually from the wide players. English team Chelsea used this system to great effect during its back-to-back Premier League title successes in 2005 and 2006.

A single striker receives and holds up the ball

Wide men join the striker in attack

A bank of four defenders provides the necessary cover in defense

4-2-3-1

This was arguably the dominant formation on either side of the millennium. It revolves around the midfield, with two of the central players in holding roles and the other one concentrating on attack. France beat Brazil 3–0 in the 1998 World Cup final using this formation. It is popular in continental Europe.

Two of the three midfielders play a defensive role

The striker relies on wide men and advanced midfielder

Four-man defense adds solidity

> **" THE 4-2-3-1** FORMATION REVOLVES AROUND THE MIDFIELD, WITH TWO OF THE **CENTRAL PLAYERS IN HOLDING ROLES**. **"**

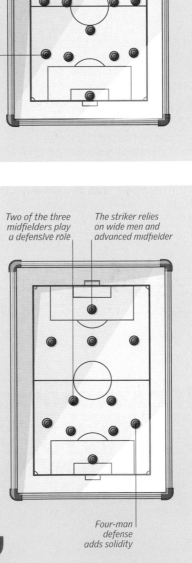

Other modern formations

While the majority of formations have been adopted as standard throughout the soccer world, others—such as *catenaccio* and "Total Soccer"—have become synonymous with a particular team or nation.

Catenaccio (1-4-3-2)

Catenaccio, which means "door bolt" in Italian, relied on a *libero*, or sweeper (see p.45) stationed in front of the goalkeeper to counter the risk of an opposing forward breaking through the main line of defense. It was fundamentally a defensive system, but by forcing opponents to commit extra players forward, it left them vulnerable to rapid counterattacks.

THE BIRTH OF CATENACCIO

Catenaccio first became popular in Italy in the late 1940s. Gipo Viani, the Salernitana manager, claimed to have invented the formation after seeing fishermen using two nets—the reserve net was used to pick up any fish that had managed to evade the first one.

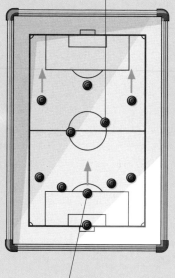

Hardworking midfielders help out in defense and have to join rapid counterattacks

The libero, or sweeper, adds an extra line of defense

CATENACCIO FORCES OPPONENTS TO **COMMIT EXTRA PLAYERS FORWARD**, LEAVING THEM **VULNERABLE** TO RAPID **COUNTERATTACKS**.

THE **CHRISTMAS TREE** IS A MORE ATTACKING **ADAPTATION OF 4-3-3**.

Total Soccer

Rinus Michels, manager of the great Ajax and Netherlands teams of the early 1970s, gave his players unprecedented freedom to tackle the game as it unfolded. Outfield players had no fixed positions, although the team had adopted a variant of 4-3-3; each player had to be prepared to occupy any position as the need arose. Although thrilling to watch, the team lost the World Cup final in 1974.

TOTAL SOCCER REBORN

The Netherlands scored the perfect Total Soccer goal, against Italy at Euro 2008, turning defense into instant attack in the blink of an eye.

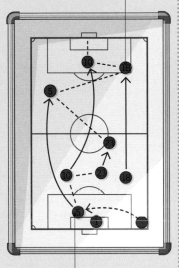

Dirk Kuyt (18) heads a pass from van Bronkhurst into the path of Sneijder, who scores

Giovanni van Bronkhurst (5) clears a corner to teammate Wesley Sneijder (10), and runs down the left flank

KEY	
●	Holland
●	Italy
--	Pass
—	Player movement

VARIATIONS

THE DIAMOND

Alf Ramsey's "wingless wonders," England, won the 1966 World Cup with this formation. It gives a side great solidity in midfield, with the full-backs providing the width in attack. AC Milan won the Champions League in 2007 playing with the same system.

THE CHRISTMAS TREE

Named after its pointed shape, the 4-3-2-1 formation is a more attacking adaptation of 4-3-3. In this setup, two players play behind a lone striker

("in the hole"). Terry Venables's England side used the Christmas Tree formation to great effect at Euro '96.

THE FUTURE: 4-6-0

At a 2003 coaching conference in Rio de Janeiro, former Brazil manager Carlos Alberto Parreira declared the 4-6-0 to be the formation of the future. His prediction seems to be coming true: Manchester United won the 2008 Champions League playing with no dedicated striker. Instead, the team relied on attacking midfielders bursting forward as and when opportunities arose.

Defensive strategies

Defenders, like all other players, need to master the basic skills of the game, such as passing and ball control, but in some departments—notably tackling—they have to be considerably better than average. Individual technical ability, though, is only part of the story. Defenders also need to address how they are going to work together as a unit.

Defending as a unit

A good defense provides the foundation for every great team, and if a defense wants to become impenetrable, it needs to become a coherent unit. That means working together to regain possession of the ball, holding a tight defensive line, claiming responsibility for marking attacking players, and disrupting the opposing side's organization as much as possible.

Holding the line

Defenders form a line across the field exactly parallel to the goal line, particularly when the opposition has possession of the ball. The line helps increase the chances of catching opposing forwards offside, unless one of them manages to cut through with a well-timed run. It also dictates how far upfield the team as a whole plays. Midfielders should base themselves slightly ahead of the defensive line. The same is true of forwards in relation to the midfielders.

KEY

● Attacking team
● Defensive team
---- Pass
— Player movement

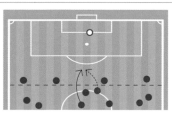

HIGH DEFENSIVE LINE
There is a danger of opponents breaking the offside trap (see box, below) with a well-timed through-ball.

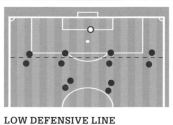

LOW DEFENSIVE LINE
There is a danger of allowing opposition players to get too close to goal.

THE OFFSIDE TRAP

Holding a good defensive line is a deterrent in itself, but the offside trap adds another level. It involves all the defenders stepping forward just before an opponent passes the ball to a forward-running striker, thus playing him offside at the moment the ball is struck (see pp.18–19). It is a high-risk strategy, but can be very effective if performed properly. The Arsenal back four of the late 1980s and early '90s were masters of the offside trap.

Marking

Marking is about preventing the ball being passed easily among the opposing team. Picking up an opponent, whether from set pieces or in open play, is one of the defender's most important tasks. If several defenders decide to mark one opponent at the same time, they will leave other opponents dangerously unmarked. There are two options to avoid this: zonal marking and man-to-man marking.

KEY
- Attacking team
- Defensive team

Zonal marking

Zonal marking was developed in the 1950s to deal with the problem of playing against a team using withdrawn strikers. Here defenders are responsible for specific areas of the field rather than particular opponents.

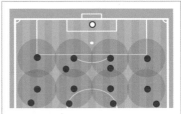

ZONAL MARKING
Players occupy an area of the field and do not directly mark an opponent.

Man-to-man marking

Man-to-man marking is simple: a defender is allocated an opponent and has to stick to him no matter where he runs. The system's advantage is its clarity. The disadvantage is that it allows crafty attacking players to pull defenders out of position.

MAN-TO-MAN
Each player has to mark a single opponent.

BOBBY MOORE

Possessing an ability to read the game as it unfolds before him, few defenders played with as much effortless grace as England's 1966 World Cup-winning captain.

Great defensive partnerships

Most formations pair two central defenders together at the back and their partnership is one of the most important on the field. It helps if they are not too similar in playing style (so they can offer more than one skill) and there are various theories about the ideal combination.

The perfect mix

One tried-and-tested formula is a ball-winner plus a ball-player, with the former doing most of the tackling and the latter picking up the ball and passing (such as Italy's Fabio Cannavaro and Alessandro Nesta). The most important ingredient is mutual understanding.

THE BEREZUTSKY TWINS

Understanding is the most important component of a defensive partnership and no two people understand each other better than identical twins. Aleksei and Vasili Berezutsky of CSKA Moscow and Russia are living proof that such a formula can work at the highest level of the sport. Born on June 20, 1982, Aleksei is the younger one, and is also half an inch (1cm) shorter. They have played together at the heart of the CSKA defense since 2002, and for the national side since 2003.

NESTA AND CANNAVARO

Cannavaro's positional sense and superb reading of the game broke up opposition attacks. Nesta, supremely quick and elegant on the ball, picked up the pieces and instigated new attacks.

TOP 5: PARTNERSHIPS
Successful teams are invariably built on the foundations of a great defensive partnership. Here are five of the finest:

BARESI AND COSTACURTA (AC MILAN)
They played together for so long in AC Milan's defense they instinctively knew where the other would be. When Baresi retired, Paolo Maldini stepped effortlessly into his shoes.

HANSEN AND LAWRENSON (LIVERPOOL)
The cornerstone of the great Liverpool team of the early 1980s, Lawrenson was the quicker, Hansen the more stylish, but both had the priceless ability to bring the ball out of defense.

ADAMS AND KEOWN (ARSENAL)
The center backs were formidable to begin with, but got even better as time passed on. Born in the same year, they won a league and FA Cup double at age 31, and another in 2002 at age 35.

LEBOEUF AND DESAILLY (CHELSEA)
A World Cup-winning center back partnership with France in 2002, Leboeuf and Desailly were also a formidable force at Chelsea.

SCHWARZENBECK AND BECKENBAUER (BAYERN MUNICH)
Beckenbauer's elegance and attacking libero style was perfectly complemented by Schwarzenbeck's no-nonsense traditional approach to the game.

Defending from the front

It's not just defenders who need to defend. Forwards today are expected to help out when their side does not have the ball. This puts pressure on the opposing defenders, and on the goalkeeper when he receives a back pass. The purpose of this is to force a defensive error and create goal-scoring opportunities.

KEY
- Attacking team A
- Defensive team B
- Action area

Condensing play
When the attacking team has possession of the ball, the defending team can make life difficult for them by quickly filling the gaps between players. Condensing the play in this way makes the field appear smaller, denies the attacking team room in which to operate efficiently, and increases the chances of forcing them to make a mistake. It is a major weapon to use when trying to regain possession of the ball.

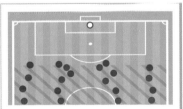

CONDENSING PLAY
Team B condenses the play, putting pressure on attacking Team A.

> **CONDENSING** THE PLAY MAKES THE **FIELD APPEAR SMALLER**, PRESSURING THE OPPONENTS INTO **MAKING MISTAKES**.

Shielding

Shielding the ball involves a player positioning his body between an opponent and the ball without actually obstructing the opponent. It is a useful skill and one that can be used all over the field, from a lone striker holding the ball up, to a defender shielding the ball from an attacker to ensure that it goes out of play for a goal-kick or a throw-in.

Facing away from the attacker, the defender protects the ball

Close control is essential when shielding

Shepherding

Just as a shepherd uses a dog to control his flock without touching them, a defender "shepherds" an attacker, trying to maneuver him away from danger zones, without ever trying to take the ball away. This tactic has two main purposes—to move attacking players away from the goal and to force them to play the ball with their weaker foot.

KEY	
●	Attacking team
●	Defensive team
—	Player movement
▨	Danger zone

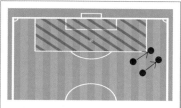

SHEPHERDING I
The defender shepherds a left-footed striker onto his weaker right foot.

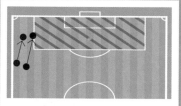

SHEPHERDING II
The defender prevents the winger from getting in a cross.

Doubling up

If an opponent becomes isolated, the defenders can dispossess him by "doubling up"—putting two defenders on one attacker. Defenders need to be careful: two defenders on one attacker means other attackers are likely to be left unguarded.

KEY	
●	Attacking team
●	Defensive team
—	Player movement

DOUBLING UP
Player C runs back to assist player B against opponent player A.

TOP 5: HARDMEN

Defensive hardmen are there to terrify opponents. A type of anti-strategy, it can be very effective. The players mentioned below can be viewed as being among the toughest players the game of soccer has ever seen.

CLAUDIO GENTILE

Gentile—"gentle" in Italian—was an inappropriate last name for one of the toughest defenders of all time. "Football (soccer) is not for ballerinas," the Juventus hardman said, after famously kicking a young Diego Maradona into submission at the 1982 World Cup. Remarkably, he never received a red card.

TOMMY SMITH

According to Bill Shankly, Smith wasn't born, he was "quarried." Smith, who enjoyed a 16-year career with Liverpool, once handed opposing striker Jimmy Greaves a piece of paper before a match. It was the lunch menu from the Liverpool Infirmary.

RONALD KOEMAN

After the Netherlands beat host West Germany in the semi-final of Euro '88, Koeman swapped his shirt with German midfielder Olaf Thon, then rudely pretended to wipe his backside with it. The great Dutch defender had a shot like a cannonball as well as a bone-crunching tackle.

DUNGA

Brazilians are not known for their hard tackling, but the captain of the 1994 World Cup-winning team played like a naval destroyer and even looked scary. Capped 91 times, he added much-needed strength to Brazil's traditionally attacking style of play.

STUART PEARCE

Known as "Psycho," the giant-thighed England fullback used to listen to the Sex Pistols to get into the right mood for matches. Pearce (left) once tried to run off a broken leg, and when Basile Boli head-butted him at Euro '92, it was the Frenchman who came off worse.

> THE DEFENSE CAN **DISPOSSESS** AN ISOLATED OPPONENT BY PUTTING **TWO DEFENDERS** ON **ONE ATTACKER**.

Attacking strategies

There are three main choices when it comes to attacking play. How many strikers do you employ? Do you try to get into a scoring position via the sides of the field ("the flanks") or through the middle? And do you seek to get there through intricate or direct passing? The answers depend on the strength of your team, the weaknesses of the opposition, and the way the game is unfolding.

Through the middle: the long-ball game

The long-ball game involves getting the ball from the defenders to the forwards as quickly as possible. This entails passing the ball two-thirds of the length of the field or more in the air, and for this reason the approach is also known as "route-one soccer."

Ideal requirements

The long-ball game works best with a tall forward (the "target man"), who is likely to win the long aerial balls, or with wingers stationed near the sidelines. Teams use this strategy to get the ball rapidly out of defense to minimize the risk of losing possession in a dangerous area, and to get the ball up to the forwards before the defending team has had a chance to organize its defense.

KEY

● Holland
● Argentina
--- Pass
— Player movement

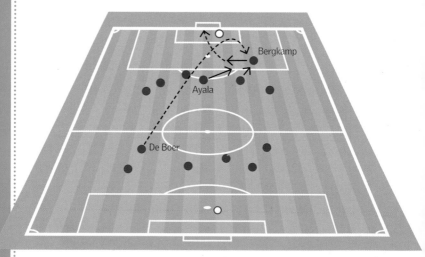

ROUTE-ONE PERFECTION
There is nothing attractive or particularly skillful about the long-ball game, but there are exceptions, such as Dennis Bergkamp's exquisite 89th-minute, match-winning goal for the Netherlands against Argentina in the 1998 World Cup quarter-finals.

Intricate passing

Well-marshaled defenders can render the long-ball game ineffective by packing the defense with extra players to leave attacking forwards hopelessly outnumbered. When teams face such a defense, they have to rely on intricate passing to break through. It helps if they have players who are skillful enough to pass the ball accurately and quickly in confined spaces.

Player movement

Static players are easy for defenders to mark. Successful intricate passing depends on attackers moving around and the player in possession of the ball anticipating his teammates' movements. The passer should also move into space as soon as he has played to provide teammates with another passing option.

Element of surprise

Tricks, such as back-heels, are invaluable in and around the penalty area. They are impossible for defenders to anticipate and can buy the attackers time and space. Ideally, all attackers will be alert to their teammates' tricks, but even if they aren't, they may still find themselves in a position to capitalize on them.

Slide-rule passes

This pass is weighted so precisely that it reaches a forward-running attacker the very moment he arrives in the desired position. It is a vital tool for breaking even the most stubborn of defenses.

SLIDE-RULE PASS
The forward takes the ball in his stride and shoots on goal.

● Attacking team
● Defensive team
---- Pass
— Player movement

> **" STATIC PLAYERS** ARE EASY FOR **DEFENDERS TO MARK. "**

PAUL SCHOLES

The attacking midfielder for Manchester United, Paul Scholes is one of the neatest passers in modern soccer.

The one-two

The one-two is an excellent way to get past a defender who is standing between the attacker (who has the ball) and the goal. It needs two attackers, one of them stationary and one running with the ball. The running attacker passes to his stationary teammate, continues to run forward past the defender, then receives the ball back from the stationary teammate. Also known as the "wall pass," the one-two is particularly effective around the edge of the penalty area.

THE ONE-TWO
Player A passes to player B, runs, and receives a return pass.

● Attacking team
● Defensive team
--- Pass/shot
— Player movement

Pressing

The pressing game involves never giving an opponent a moment's rest when their team has the ball, thereby pressurizing them into making an error. In the modern game, all players are expected to press, including the forwards, who are expected to harry an opponent's goalkeeper and central defenders.

Probing

If a team is comfortable in possession, there is no need to rush into an all-out attack. Instead, they can "probe" their opponents' defense and frustrate them. The attacking team can keep passing the ball between themselves until a clear shooting opportunity presents itself.

❝ COUNTER-ATTACK CAN PLACE **HUGE PRESSURE** ON THE OPPONENTS' **DEFENSE**. ❞

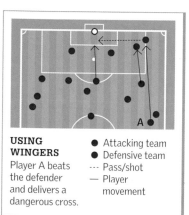

USING WINGERS
Player A beats the defender and delivers a dangerous cross.

● Attacking team
● Defensive team
--- Pass/shot
— Player movement

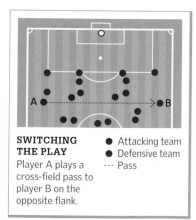

SWITCHING THE PLAY
Player A plays a cross-field pass to player B on the opposite flank.

● Attacking team
● Defensive team
--- Pass

USING THE FLANKS
Instead of playing through the middle, teams use wide players who have pace, dribbling skills, the ability to run past defenders, and put in accurate crosses.

SWITCHING THE ATTACK
If one side of the field presents a better attacking proposition, the team in possession can "switch the play," and focus on the less well-defended side.

ESTEBAN CAMBIASSO

The Argentine midfielder celebrates scoring one of the greatest goals in World Cup history. Scored against Serbia in 2006, the goal was a masterclass on build-up play and included all the key attacking strategies.

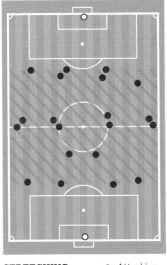

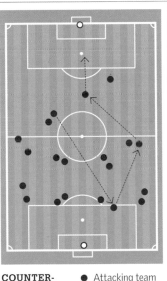

STRETCHING PLAY
The attacking team increases the distance between its players.

● Attacking team
● Defensive team
\\\ Action area

COUNTER-ATTACKS
An intercepted pass in defense can lead to an instant attack.

● Attacking team
● Defensive team
--- Pass
— Player movement

STRETCHING PLAY

Just as teams condense play during defense (see p.151), they stretch the play in attack by increasing the distance between its players to create space.

COUNTERATTACKING

An instant switch from defense to attack, this strategy can place huge pressure on an opponent's defense. A few players must stay upfield during an opposition attack.

Set pieces

Set pieces are free-kicks, corners, and throw-ins. About 30 percent of goals are scored directly or indirectly from set-piece situations, so they are extremely important for both the attacking and defending side. Modern teams spend hours practicing, creating, and honing set-piece routines, from both an attacking and defensive point of view.

Corners: the defending team

Although a defending team has no idea what kind of corner an attacking side will deliver, it should always follow certain principles such as adopting a marking strategy (be it zonal or man-to-man marking, see p.154) and putting a man on the inside of each of the goal posts.

Marking

Tactics vary depending on whether a team uses zonal or man-to-man marking, but the basic principle is to stick to your man and stay goal-side of him. If a defender lets the attacker get in front of him, the latter will have a chance to direct a header on goal.

WHAT SHOULD THE GOALKEEPER DO?

A goalkeeper has two main choices: to come and meet the ball (either by catching or punching it) or to stay on his goal line and hope to make a save. It requires excellent judgment to decide what to do in the heat of the moment.

Guarding the posts

The defending team should place one man on each post. As the ball comes in, they need to position themselves on the goal line, just inside the post they are guarding. If they do this, they will be ready to clear any goal attempts heading for the inside of their posts.

❝ WHEN DEFENDING DURING CORNERS, ALWAYS STICK TO YOUR MAN AND STAY ON THE GOAL-SIDE OF HIM. ❞

Corners: the attacking team

A corner provides an attacking team with a fantastic opportunity to create a goal-scoring chance. Numerous moves have been devised over the years—some more innovative than others—all of which fall into one of the three categories: a short corner, a near-post corner, or a far-post corner.

Short corners

Unlike a standard corner, no attempt is made to cross the ball directly into the penalty area; instead the corner-taker makes a short pass to a teammate, moves into an onside position, receives the ball back, and only then delivers his cross. The goal is to confuse the defenders' plans.

KEY	
●	Attacking team
●	Defensive team
----	Pass/cross
—	Player movement

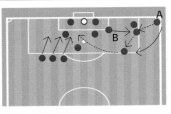

SHORT CORNERS
Player B comes for the ball, then returns it to player A who crosses it.

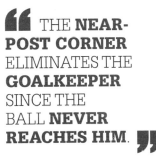

THE NEAR-POST CORNER ELIMINATES THE **GOALKEEPER** SINCE THE BALL **NEVER REACHES HIM**.

Near-post corners

A near-post corner is played to the goal post nearest the taker. It eliminates the goalkeeper, since the ball does not reach him. An attacking player is stationed on the near post who heads the ball, hoping an incoming teammate will pick it up and score.

Far-post corners

A far-post corner is played to the goal post that is farthest away from the taker. The goal is to bypass the goalkeeper. The ball is struck with pace and the plan is for a teammate to escape his marker, meet the ball, and score.

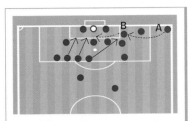

NEAR-POST CORNER
Player A crosses the ball to player B, who flicks the ball on for teammates.

FAR-POST CORNER
Attackers try to avoid their markers in order to score from the deeper corner.

Free-kicks: the defending team

Because free-kicks provide an opponent with an ideal opportunity to shoot on goal, it is vital that defenses are organized to deal with the impending threat. Every defender needs to be on his guard. Marking (zonal or man-to-man) needs to be tight, and then a wall needs to be created that directly blocks the route to goal.

Defensive walls

To defend a free-kick, the goalkeeper sets up the defensive wall. He may have only one member or as many as five. The goalkeeper needs to ensure that one side of the goal is covered, allowing him to concentrate on the other side.

Anticipating free-kicks

Defenders need to be alert to quickly taken free-kicks or ones delivered to an unmarked opponent. If the free-kick is indirect, a player should be nominated to close the ball down as soon as it has been touched by an opponent.

Free-kicks: the attacking team

Some free-kicks awarded in advanced positions invite crosses, in which case—because the ball is crossed into the box—the tactics for both sides are similar to those in the corners section (see pp.108–09). Others provide opportunities for a direct shot on goal.

Rehearsed free-kicks

Rehearsed free-kicks range from simple taps to the side to complex passing routines. All have the same intention: to catch an opponent unawares. Argentina showcased a perfectly executed free-kick against England at the 1998 World Cup (see below). In a move honed on the training ground, Gabriel Batistuta made a dummy run, Javier Zanetti peeled into space from behind the defensive wall, was found by Juan Sebastian Veron, shot, and scored.

FREE-KICK TRICKS
Javier Zanetti positioned himself behind England's defensive wall.

KEY
- Attacking team
- Defensive team
- ---- Pass/cross
- — Player movement

" FREE-KICKS PROVIDE THE ATTACKING TEAM WITH AN IDEAL **GOAL-SCORING OPPORTUNITY**. "

THE DEFENSIVE WALL

The number of players in a wall depends on the area of the field from which a free-kick is taken. It will range from one player to five.

Managers and coaches

Soccer vocabulary is packed with military terminology. A season is often described as a "campaign," a match a "battle." In this spirit, a team can be called an army. If the players are the troops led by a captain, the coach is the drill sergeant and the manager is the general.

The modern manager

The role of the modern manager was defined first in the late 1920s and early 1930s. Prior to this, boardroom directors handled squads and players determined tactics.

ARSÈNE WENGER

Arsenal's Arsène Wenger has been managing the North London club for over a decade, a rarity in the modern game.

THE MANAGER'S RESPONSIBILITIES

The 21st-century soccer manager has to juggle a bewildering number of tasks. The following are just a handful of them.

TEAM AND PLAYERS
- Team selection
- Motivating the players
- Deciding on formations
- Making substitutions
- Giving team talks

BEHIND THE SCENES
- Signing new players
- Maintaining player discipline
- Overseeing player development
- Setting coaching policy
- Scouting for new players

RUNNING THE CLUB
- Appointing ancillary staff
- Delegating responsibilities
- Attending board meetings
- Setting coaching policy
- Scouting for new players

IN THE SPOTLIGHT
- Dealing with the media
- Preparing program notes
- Helping club sponsors
- Attending club functions
- Appearing on club's TV channel

THE GREAT MANAGERS

A number of managers have achieved unparalleled success in the game, but here are perhaps the ten best managers ever to have taken charge of a team.

HERBERT CHAPMAN

The man who invented and personified the idea of the modern, autocratic, media-savvy manager, he won titles with Huddersfield and Arsenal.

SIR ALEX FERGUSON

Ferguson took his grit and cunning to Aberdeen and led the team to the top of Scottish soccer. He then headed south and transformed Manchester United into England's dominant club.

BELA GUTTMANN

The Hungarian is the only coach to have won the European Cup and the Copa Libertadores—with Benfica and Peñarol respectively—and was a key figure in bringing tactical innovations to Latin America.

HELENIO HERRERA

The man they called "The Magician" conjured up titles and trophies at Barcelona and Inter Milan with his mix of lock-tight defense and surreal motivational techniques.

RINUS MICHELS

"Iron" Rinus brought discipline and coherence to Dutch soccer, turned Ajax into a global force with his Total Soccer (see p.149), and coached the Dutch national side to Euro '88 success.

BOB PAISLEY

Twenty years in the famous Liverpool "boot room" before he became the club's manager, Bob Paisley may have appeared avuncular, but he ruled Anfield with a rod of iron and won six league titles and three European Cups.

BILL SHANKLY

Shankly's Liverpool teams delighted, his words inspired, and his memory is treasured. No other coach has been hoisted into and across the Spion Kop stand in scenes of jubilation the way he has been.

VITTORIO POZZO

Pozzo brought modern soccer management to Italy and defined its role there. He enjoyed success with Torino, but two World Cup wins and an Olympic gold for Italy are hard to beat.

BRIAN CLOUGH

Erratic and volcanic, Clough was also magnificent and inspirational. To take a small club like Nottingham Forest to two consecutive European Cup wins was a feat unparalleled in soccer management anywhere.

GIOVANNI TRAPATTONI

In the excruciating hothouse of Italian soccer, one man stays cool: Trapattoni won it all with Juventus in the 1980s and again with Bayern Munich in the 1990s.

The anatomy of a club

Since Sheffield FC was established in northern England in 1857, the club has been at the center of soccer cultures all over the world. But clubs come in many shapes and sizes, and methods of ownership have changed, too. In England, clubs moved from being private organizations to private limited companies. Social clubs emerged in southern Europe and Latin America. In communist societies, state organizations and trade unions ran teams.

Types of club ownership

A soccer club is no longer solely represented by 11 players taking to a field up to twice a week wearing a familiar uniform; the modern club extends far beyond the confines of the sidelines. It is a business, a potential vehicle for political advancement, and in some cases even a rich man's toy. Clubs have evolved in various ways in different parts of the world.

PRIVATE LIMITED COMPANIES
The standard form of professional soccer club in Britain, with one or many private shareholders. For many years directors were not allowed to take anything but a tiny profit out of the club. In recent years, these restrictions have been lifted and most clubs are run as medium-sized private businesses.

THE SOCIO MODEL
In Latin America and southern Europe, the original sports/social clubs out of which so many teams grew left a legacy in which all members have an annual vote for the elected officers of the club's board. The club itself can neither be bought nor sold.

OTHER TYPES OF CLUB
In France and Germany, soccer clubs are owned and controlled by the original amateur associations out of which they grew. In the US, Australia, and Mexico, franchises run clubs. A new development has been the e-club, where anyone can buy a stake in the club.

FC UNITED OF MANCHESTER
When American tycoon Malcolm Glazer acquired a controlling interest in Manchester United in May 2005, supporters who opposed the takeover decided to form their own club. FC United entered the tenth tier of English soccer in the fall of 2005.

> **" THE MODERN CLUB EXTENDS FAR BEYOND THE CONFINES OF THE SIDELINES; IT IS A BUSINESS. "**

Who's in charge?

The power and managerial structures in soccer clubs are an endless source of intrigue. The relationships between presidents, coaches, technical directors, and directors of soccer serve to create as much friction as they do cooperation and have generated as many newspaper headlines in recent years as the action on the field.

TRADITIONAL SET-UP
The classic set-up that hinges on an all-powerful manager who takes charge of all aspects of the first team, scouting, and youth development.

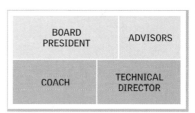

ALL-POWERFUL TECHNICAL DIRECTOR
The coach can ask the technical director for certain players, but final decisions on the transfer policy lie with the director.

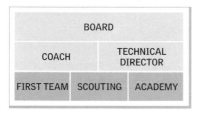

CLASSIC CONTINENTAL
In this, the club is run by the board, the technical director (responsible for dealings on the transfer market), and the coach (responsible for first team affairs).

PRESIDENTIAL CONTROL
The board president, assisted by a number of advisers, calls all the shots, from team selection to transfer policy. The coach answers only to the president.

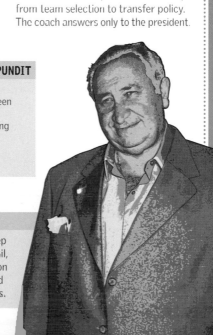

PRESIDENT, PRIME MINISTER, AND PUNDIT
Italian prime minister Silvio Berlusconi bought AC Milan in 1986. He was often seen bemoaning his manager Carlo Ancelotti's tactics. The manager's insistence on playing 4-3-2-1 was a constant source of anguish for Berlusconi, who believes that soccer is a game requiring two strikers.

JESUS GIL Y GIL
Money and power just can't keep away from soccer. Jesus Gil Y Gil, wanted in courts across Spain on corruption, kept Atlético Madrid in the headlines for two decades.

Index

A

unclassified strikers 57
withdrawn striker 54,
151
fouls 12, 20–21
and free-kick *see* free-kick
and sliding tackle 44
free-kick
anticipating 162
and attacking team 163
"banana shot" (Carlos) 17
corner-kick
see corner-kick
curving 111, 112–13
and defensive wall 111,
112, 162–63
dipping 112
direct 16, 17, 20, 22,
110
hand signals 22
indirect 16, 20, 22, 110
penalty spot 110
quick 111
rehearsed 163
rules 13
as set piece 14
skills 110–11, 162–63
tactical heading 103
freestyle skills
around the world 132
and Capoeira martial art
131
head stall 130
keepy-uppie 130, 132
rainbow 131
tournaments 132–33
futsal, goal size 37

global styles 140–41
goal, construction
requirements 36–37, 39
goal scoring
and corner-kick
109–10
and free-kick *see* free-kick
and throw-in 107
goal-kick
and goal area 38
hand signal 22
rules 13, 24
goalkeeper
angle, narrowing 119
catching ball 124
crosses, dealing with
124
defenders, marshalling 43,
125
and distribution method
122–23
diving save 121
grounding ball 120
half-volley distribution
123
impeding 16
"M" hand position 118
overarm throw distribution
123
and penalty-kick *see*
penalty-kick
protective gear 31–33
punching ball 124
punt distribution 43, 123
referee monitoring 24
role and skills 42–43,
118–23
roll out distribution 123
"scorpion kick" (Higuita)
43, 125
shirt 29
shot-stopping 118
stance and body position
118
"W" hand position
118

Gomes, Élton Jose Xavier
62
Grobbelaar, Bruce 114
Guttmann, Bela 165

H
halfway line 39
hand signals 22, 25, 110
Hansen, Alan 153
hardmen 155
heading
and ball control 73
basic 102
defensive 104
diving 105
far-post 103
flick 103
forwards 52
near-post 103
skills 102–05
tactical and corner-kick
103
Henry, Thierry 55
Herrera, Helenio 165
Higuita, René 43, 125
Hunter, Norman 46

I
injuries and rehabilitation
134–35
international games
global styles 140–41
field dimension 39
Inzaghi, Pippo 55
Italian style 141

J
James, David 65
Jennings, Pat
63, 126

G
Garnier, Arnaud 133
Gentile, Claudio 152
Gerrard, Steven 99
Giggs, Ryan 65
Gil Y Gil, Jesus 167
Glazer, Malcolm 166

Acknowledgments

Dorling Kindersley would like to thank the following people for their help in the preparation of this book: Mikhail Sipovich at Colours Of Football and Paul Wootton, for input on the artworks; Adam Brackenbury for creative technical support; and Margaret McCormack for indexing.

Picture credits

The publisher would like to thank the following for their kind permission to use their photographs for artists' reference:

(Key: b-below/bottom; c-center; l-left; r-right; t-top; tr-top right; tl-top left; cr-center right, cl-center left; br-bottom right; bl-bottom left)

Corbis: Carmen Jaspersen/epa 89br; Christopher Courtois/epa 134–35; Geoff Caddick/epa 100–01; Leo Mason 92; Sygma 167; **Getty Images:** 10, 17, 26, 42bl, 43bl, 47, 51, 53, 54, 57, 60–61, 73bl, 74tr, 74br, 75bl, 75br, 79, 84, 104, 125, 138, 151, 154, 155, 164; AFP 2–3, 42br, 55, 116, 133, 106, 62bl (Crouch), 68, 72–73t, 165; Andersen Ross 13; Bob Thomas 63br (Pele), 159; Bongarts 24, 43br, 62br (Maradona), 75tl, 78, 162–63; Clive Brunskill 14tr; EMPICS Sport 43t; Fox Photos 80t; Garrett Ellwood / MLS 72br; Man Utd 70; MLS 112–13; Popperfoto 122, 63bl (Foulkes), 152l, 152r, 157; Scott Pribyl / MLS 73br; STF / AFP 90

All other images © Dorling Kindersley

For further information see:
www.dkimages.com